A Mingled Yarn

 FriesenPress

One Printers Way
Altona, MB R0G 0B0
Canada

www.friesenpress.com

ISBN
978-1-03-917708-6 (Hardcover)
978-1-03-917707-9 (Paperback)
978-1-03-917709-3 (eBook)

1. BIOGRAPHY & AUTOBIOGRAPHY, ENTERTAINMENT & PERFORMING ARTS

Distributed to the trade by The Ingram Book Company

A Mingled Yarn

Dolores for ever one of the best audiences

[signature]

By Nick Hutchinson
with James Fagan Tait

"Nine years ago, over an early morning coffee, Nick asked me to help him with his book. I would go up to Enderby between gigs, record, transcribe, adapt, and re-edit. Nine years later, poof! A book! I'm grateful to Nick for sharing his story with me, and I'm a different person for knowing it."

James Fagan Tait is an actor, director, and playwright based in Vancouver. He is the recipient of two *Jessie Richardson Awards*. He has worked with director *Nick Hutchinson* in five shows at the *Caravan Farm Theatre*.

The webbe of our life, is of a mingled yarne,
good and ill together: our vertues would be proud,
if our faults whipt them not, and our crimes would dispaire
if they were not cherish'd by our vertues

William Shakespeare, *All's Well That Ends Well*

Excerpt from a letter to my grandson Chay, the day after he was born, February 21, 2008:

Here's a story that I want to tell you. It's called *A Mingled Yarn*. What, you may ask, is a yarn? The good old dictionary says: "a twisted strand of fiber used for knitting or weaving," and when it comes to sea and ships, "bundles of fibers twisted together which are then twisted into bundles to form strands and finally are twisted or plaited to form rope."

And then a third meaning: "a story, a tale especially one that is incredible , spinning a yarn, a tall tale, weaving a tapestry."

And this yarn is all about strands, threads, strings that weave together to be made into something.

A rope? A ladder? A life . . . ?

Contents

Fyodor Petrovich Komissarzhevsky, 1832 – 1905

Konstantin Stanislavski, 1863 – 1938

Fyodor Fyodorovich Komissarzhevsky, 1882 – 1954

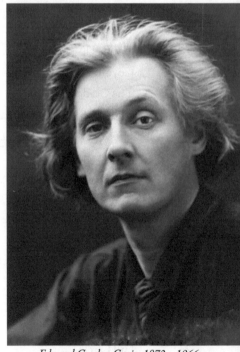

Edward Gordon Craig, 1872 – 1966

Ghosts

These ghosts loom across this yarn, for they are the fundamental architects of the extraordinary theatre time that I've been lucky enough to experience. Oh dear, would that they could resurrect and put theatre back in the centre of culture before it becomes a lost art.

But if you don't care for ghosts, you can always skip to Chapter One!

I'm living in my dirty little trailer in Dunster, in northern BC. It's 2005, when I get an email from my great friend Dinah Casson. She's just been hired by a Russian oligarch to build a Stanislavsky "interactive museo lobby" for his newest acquisition, the old factory that spun the gold and silver thread for the Tsar's army and belonged to Stanislavsky. Who knew that Stanislavsky, apart from being perhaps the greatest innovator of modern theatre, was one of the richest men in Moscow? The oligarch is going to renovate the old factory into a state-of-the-art business meeting place for Gazprom and other major Russian-owned global enterprises. The project is going to be dedicated to Stanislavsky who, for the oligarch, embodies the ultimate integration of business and art.

Dinah is starting her work by asking a number of people what Stanislavsky means to them. Sitting in the northern wilds of BC, surrounded by my horses, and elk, and coyotes, he doesn't mean much. When I was first getting into theatre and directing, he meant so much more. My Mum had given me Stanislavsky's *My Life in Art* and his incredible mise en scène of *The Seagull*, which I'd worked with extensively. But beyond that, I couldn't think of much more to say, so I left it for a couple of days.

And then, while I was sorting out some books, I moved a pile of *The Mask* magazine (the work of revolutionary theatre visionary Gordon Craig, which my grandmother had given to me), and out fell the proverbial package of letters. I sat down on the bed and started to read through the letters. They were from Gordon Craig to my grandparents, Mary and Jack Hutchinson, from Moscow between 1908 and 1911. I put two and two together and thought, *Oh my God, he was doing his famous* Hamlet *production with Stanislavsky at the Moscow Arts Theatre.* I consulted my theatre history books: his *Hamlet* opened in Moscow, January eighth, 1912.

Ever since I was a boy, my grandmother had showered me with woodcuts, pictures, and books by Gordon Craig. She recognized that I was in the same boat as he: he was the son of the great actress Ellen Terry, in the same way that I was the son of the great actress Peggy Ashcroft. His production of *Hamlet* with Stanislavsky was the "crack-open" of the modern theatre. Stanislavsky was beginning to mean more to me, and I became involved in Dinah's project.

During the course of the research, I noticed that the name Komisarjevsky kept cropping up. My mother had married a Komis before I was born, but I knew next to nothing about him. The research revealed that Komisarjevsky's father was a great opera singer, and to make extra money on the side, he would give piano lessons to young daughters of rich fathers, one of whom he ran off with to Italy, leaving a wife and two daughters in St Petersburg. There in Italy was born my mum's second husband, Komis. (He was named exactly the same as his father, so to avoid confusion let's use his nickname, Komis.)

The dad eventually came back to Moscow and to whom should he give singing lessons? A young Stanislavsky. Stanislavsky wanted to be an opera singer, but his smoking stood in the way. However, the two men enjoyed each other's company and were fascinated with the theatre.

Under Komisarjevsky's mentorship, they formed the Moscow Opera Society and produced many operas and plays and Stanislavsky acted and directed. This led, eventually, to the Moscow Arts Theatre.

These are threads. Strands.

Komis, the son, came back to Russia from Italy, as an architect, and ultimately became a successful theatre and opera director in his own right. He had a respectful if not entirely comfortable relationship with his father's friend, Stanislavsky. He woke up one day in 1920, in his post revolution, rat-infested Moscow apartment, to Russian Secret Police knocking on his door and decided, *I need a holiday. I've got to get out of here. I'm going back to Italy.* He went through a host of near-death experiences escaping from Russia and finally ended up in England with nothing at all, and somehow or other, in a pub, he ran into John Gielgud, Alec Guinness, and Peggy Ashcroft. He started a pocket theatre over the river in Barnes, near London, and there he staged *The Seagull*—the first authentic English Chekhov—with Gielgud's company, finally revealing to the English how Chekhov should be done. He established a great, long-lasting relationship with Gielgud, seduced, married, and divorced my mother, and was hired at Stratford where he produced the most revolutionary Shakespeare anyone had ever seen. Komis' very last show was Midsummer Nights Dream in a Montreal Park.

Years later, I was at a talk with Peter Brook in Montreal. Somebody asked him if he'd ever had a mentor. He said, "Not really. I just went and did it all. There was, however, one person who I will never forget and that was Komisarjevsky [Komis] and his Shakespeare productions at Stratford."

One of the directors who saw the famous *Hamlet* in Moscow was Jacques Copeau, whose theatre in France cleared out the naturalistic paraphernalia and reintroduced the bare stage, the *traiteau nu*, and the mask. His nephew, Michel St Denis, took England by storm when his Compagnie de Quinze brought Obey's *Noah*, reflecting all of his uncle's influences. He stayed in England to stage the next great Chekhov production of *The Three Sisters* with my mum and the same company that did *The Seagull*. Michel focussed on training. He synthesized elements of Stanislavsky with elements of mask and physical training, and it, too, was revolutionary.

A few years ago, my sister Eliza pulled a book off my dad's bookshelf and said, "You should look at this. No one ever told us about this?"

Michael St. Denis, 1897 – 1971

The book told the story of how, during the war, Michel ran the Free French radio, broadcast from the BBC to France—the voice of the Resistance. He gathered about him a little troupe and ran it like a theatre company. The youngest in the troupe was none other than Pierre Lefèvre, who was to become my teacher. When the Blitz descended on London, and the troupe had to find a place to live, they were offered this charming house in Regent's Park, which belonged to a barrister—my grandfather, Jack—and his wife, Mary.

Michel was a great friend of Peggy's and a great inspiration when I was trying to find my feet in the theatre. His last enterprise was the founding of the National Theatre School of Canada.

In these ghostly weaves, there is an arc from East to West. That's my arc too.

Peggy Ashcroft and Jeremy Hutchinson, married in 1940

CHAPTER 1

To Begin at the Beginning

My first memory ever was waking up at the age of one and a half and smelling the fur coat that enfolded me. It belonged to my mum, Peggy, returned from New York, where she had given seven hundred and eighty-seven performances with Robert Morley of *Edward, My Son*, her first commercial hit. She'd gone reluctantly, leaving me and my sister in the care of Nan who had just joined the family. Nan was my alternate mum, diaper-changing-feeding-nursing-putting-to-bed-bathing mum. Peggy had come back with a fur coat, and I can still remember its smell. My first memory of my father is the comforting smell of his tweed suit which he only wore on weekends. One forgets how important smells are to children. On the occasional transatlantic phone calls, I would repeatedly say to her, "Come home to Mummy's Tiny Man," because the first song I learned was:

Tiny Man what are you doing down this way
You know that it's too far to go for little boys to play
Your Mummy will be crying, your Daddy he will scold
Go home Tiny Man and do as you are told.

By the time I'm three and no longer a tiny man, life became a struggle with the injustice of having a sister who is five years older. This was a serious problem in my life. She always got to do all these things that I never could. But of course, I was the spoiled child; I was the boy, so I probably didn't do so badly. I did develop a serious crush on Nan, my Scots nanny, to the point where I became a Conservative Party supporter, which was not really what the household expected. Later on, I insisted on wearing a kilt to any special occasion. Some of my best photos are in a kilt. I felt slightly guilty, because I wasn't really a Scot, even though I could sing every song by Harry Lauder and a number of other Scottish tunes that we played on the wind-up gramophone. The other thing that I really wanted to do was to have a drink of wine because I never was allowed. I had to be satisfied with ginger beer, which I slugged back from my highchair at Sunday lunch. I had to bide my time for wine.

I saw my mum sometimes in the morning, but she'd get up late and then she'd be gone to rehearse and then perform. So, I mostly saw her Sundays. And

my dad, Jeremy, would be gone by
breakfast time with his briefcase
and wig-box to chambers and the
Old Bailey, where he was fast rising
to be a stellar defence advocate.
The good times with my dad, apart
from Saturdays and Sundays, were
bedtimes—lots of stories. Saturday
was the big day with him—
adventures, cricket, sailing, and fun.
Sunday was a bit more ritualistic,
Sunday lunch being the key event
and delicious. But everything
would subside thereafter, with
Peggy and Jeremy buried in the
Sunday newspapers spread across
the drawing room. Later in the day,
school loomed, and Jeremy would
be holed up preparing his next
week's briefs. I didn't like Sundays.

Nick Hutchinson, 3 years old , 1949

There was only ever one exception
to the Sunday ritual. One Sunday,
my mother took me by the hand and walked me up to the Hampstead church.
The congregation started singing a hymn that had a "Halleluja" in the chorus.
My sister and I loved singing with Peggy at the piano. I knew "Halleluja"
very well and, always ready to join in a good singsong, belted out "Halleluja,
I'm a bum, halleluja, bum again"—part of the chorus of a song from the
Depression—which was not exactly to the taste of this Hampstead Anglican
congregation. My mum, partly embarrassed and partly amused, grabbed me by
the arm and hauled me away. And that was the last trip to church until much
later in life. I can't remember what I felt at the time, but later, I considered the
singing of the rousing Depression chorus in church as a badge of honour.

The other important person in my life was Ernest Squires. Squires was a
totally wonderful and delightful "manservant," odd-job man, able to run a
dinner party, and would come and work in the afternoons and do all the heavy
lifting, mowing of lawns, polishing of the silver, and anything that was beyond
the capacities of an upper-middle-class household. He was the most cheerful,
generous, enjoyable Cockney, with great energy and much fun to be around.
Many an afternoon was spent in the kitchen with Nan and Squires and us kids,
chitting and chatting. He was the other dad. So, I had these two mother-father-
servant people, just like in the old days, and blessed was I to have such cool ones.

On a beach in Dorset, Peggy met a wonderful family called the Robinsons. Stanley, the patriarch, was a well-known numismatist (authority on coins) and his wife, Pamela, was a painter, horsewoman, and mother of five, and grandmother to a growing multitude of grandkids. They became great friends. In fact, Peggy and Jeremy had honeymooned close by the Robinsons' funky old house, The Rookery, at Burton Bradstock in Dorset. And occasionally we would rent a house nearby on the cliffs for the summer holidays. My dad had a blue Sunbeam Talbot with a takey-down roof. We called it Blueskie. One day, while Squires was mowing the lawn, I went out the gate and got into Blueskie. I let the handbrake off, and it started to roll towards the edge of the cliff—I wasn't quite sure whether I was going in the right direction because, being quite small, I couldn't really see out of the windscreen. I looked over my shoulder and Squires was leaping the wall in one deft motion. He hung onto the bumper and stopped the car. That was the first of my near-death experiences. And I owe that life to Squires. Of course at the time, I was barely aware of how close a shave it had been, but the looks on the adults' faces left me in no doubt that I'd caused extreme alarm.

Meanwhile, either a little earlier or a little later than that incident, my dad was on the beach with us . . . and I don't really remember this, I've been told about it. A little boy got swept out in the undertow of the sea and everybody on the beach was yelling, but nobody was moving a muscle. Jeremy dashed into the sea, swam out and got the little boy, and handed him over to the human chain of those who by now were ready to help. Totally exhausted, Jeremy finally washed up on the beach. Nobody paid him any attention. Ever since then, he never wanted to go swimming—not because he was frightened of swimming, I don't think, but he just didn't want to go in the sea anymore. And I guess it was his second near-death experience; in the Second World War he was in oil-soaked water for however many hours, clinging to a raft, when his ship went down.

The first time I went to the theatre was to watch Peggy rehearse *Twelfth Night* at the Old Vic, which was being refurbished after the bombings of the war. I can remember the auditorium was almost done up, and the great chandelier was being readied to be hung. Peggy was rehearsing a scene with an actor who looked exactly like her—who was of course playing Sebastian, the twin of her role, Viola. And it was Pierre Lefèvre, my future mentor. I was four and most deeply impressed by the scale of the auditorium. I marveled at the close-up view of the massive glass chandelier waiting to be raised.

When I was five, I started to go to the theatre proper. First, *South Pacific* with Mary Martin, to whom I was introduced after the show at the stage door. What really inspired me in that show was one of the sailors who could roll the ship tattoed on his tummy. The second play was *The Winter's Tale* with John Gielgud and Diana Wynyard. Diana was Peggy's greatest friend. I remember us going back to "Johnny's" dressing room and he said, "What did you think of it?" And I said, "Well, Shakespeare must've been a very jokey man. He makes you laugh and cry at the same time."

And then I got a *Complete Works of Shakespeare* from Gielgud at my next birthday.

I started school when I was five. I was raring to go, and I was getting really bored at home. And of course, by that time I'd figured out reading, and I really enjoyed learning things by heart. I remember sitting in the school on the first day, and all the children and their mothers having nervous breakdowns around me at the coming separations. But I was already used to separation, and I remember just sitting there smugly getting on with my puzzle. Early in my career at school we used to lie down on blankets for a nap in the afternoon, and I had my first snog with this lovely girl whose father was the editor of my favourite kid's magazine, *The Lion*. There is something about a kiss at five or six, without any sexual overtones, that is indescribably delicious.

Euphemia Gibb, "Nan"

The other thing that I seriously remember about school was a big school party. I had come home for lunch and Nan had insisted on a nap, which I knew would be too long. Nan and I got on a bus to go back to the party, and when we got there, of course, it was all over. This ruined parties for me for the rest of my life.

In Hampstead, down towards Swiss Cottage, was The Hall, the second school in my educational career. We had to wear pink blazers with black trim and a black Maltese cross and a pink hat with black piping. It was a very odd uniform. And grey pants. That's what's called in England a "prep" school because it preps you for your secondary school. If you're in the private education stream, a prep school prepares you for your common entrance exam, which gets you into a private school—which in England is called, somewhat confusingly, a "public" school. I was "put down" for Westminster to be a weekly boarder, so I wouldn't be that far away from home, and I'd be able to come back for the weekends. (You have to be "put down" on the schools' list years ahead of time in order to get into a public school in England. There's a long list of people with money who want to send their kids to these schools.) But by the time I was twelve, I decided I wanted to go to school in Dorset instead of Westminster. I wanted to be in the country, and I knew, subconsciously, that things were not as they should be at home—there was tension in the air, my parents rarely together, my sister frequently upset for no apparent reason. I knew a little bit about the school Bryanston because our friends, the Robinsons, had come into an enormous amount of money from the family's paper bag industry, and had leased an extraordinary grand country house in Stepleton, near the school. I wanted to go to Bryanston, so I had to persuade my parents that it was a good idea.

Ernest Squires

They weren't too difficult about that, but I had to get a scholarship because I wasn't "put down" for the school. For a scholarship, you had to sit an exam for Bryanston, which was difficult. I think I got the scholarship mainly because I made the headmaster laugh when he asked me what I wanted to be when I grew up. I said, "Oh, I want to be a sheep farmer in New Zealand." He roared with laughter. He said, "I can just see you playing your guitar to your sheep. Ha ha ha ha ha!" (I had told him I played the guitar.)

Anyway, I think that scored me points. I was twelve going on thirteen.

Between the ages of five and twelve, I developed a total passion for cricket; by the age of eleven or twelve my passion was at its max.

And that's what I used to do with my dad—go to cricket matches. I'd do training in "the nets" in the winter holidays, and I became the captain of my cricket team at school. I was never very good. But I was very keen. And I had extraordinarily good style. I could play à la so-and-so and à la so-and-so because I could see and feel how so-and-so played.

And of course, that was what you did as a boy in those days with your buddy if he was also a cricket fiend—you would play "international matches," and you would bowl as so-and-so to so-and-so, and you would do the whole game. It was a big thing because it was also the heyday of cricket in England.

There were summer holidays at Stepleton in Dorset and other summer holidays at Stratford because Peggy was acting there for the season. There was a big house for the stars, Avon Cliff, with little flats for other actors. You could swim in the river Avon, and then you'd play cricket on

Grandmother Mary Hutchinson

the big, beautiful lawn. Peggy got so turned on about my cricketing that she got together a women's team of the actresses at Stratford, and they played the men in a really great match. Peggy became so cricket-crazy that she was known to go on stage with a small transistor in her costume so she wouldn't miss the vital moments of a test match.

The highlight of our cricket passion was when Peggy was made a Dame in 1956. She'd made a connection with Len Hutton, the greatest batsman of England, who was to be knighted on the same day as her. He had made the highest score ever, and he was one sweet Yorkshireman. He came to lunch with his family, and we played cricket in the garden. He knocked the ball into the neighbour's greenhouse and broke a window.

The great thing about Len Hutton was that he illuminated the issue of class for me. In the fifties, there were two classes of players, amateurs and professionals. They used different changing rooms: one had their initials in front of their name and one of them had them after. The "amateurs" were the wealthy who went to Oxford and Cambridge and private schools, and the "professionals" were the commoners and paid to play. And somewhere around this time, there was outrage in England amongst the upper classes when the English selectors chose Len Hutton as captain. "A professional as a captain of England?!" The amateurs were the upper class. They could afford to play. They played for fun, and they were always the captains. And at Lords—the shrine of cricket, the cathedral of cricket—there's an incredible pavilion which belongs to the members of the Marylebone Cricket Club, to which you become a member when you're rich and want to watch cricket. You have a lovely bar, and you can go and play old-fashioned tennis there. The players all come through the pavilion to walk out to the pitch. The members sit outside the pavilion down the steps that lead to the wicket, where there's a little white fence with a gate. And the tradition was that when the English captain comes out to bat in a test match (international match) through the pavilion, everybody rises to their feet and gives them a standing ovation all the way to the stumps. That is what you did. And when Len Hutton came out to bat . . . total silence. The fuckers sat on their hands. Can you imagine? To me, that just sized up everything about England that I unconsciously loathed. But he soldiered on and was eventually knighted on the same day as Peggy was made a Dame.

We were of the professional classes. Actors were allowed into the upper classes because they were actors. And you had actors who were more upper class than others. My dad's dad was a barrister. They were professionals. But that meant that you still belonged to the Garrick Club, to all those things that other people don't belong to. But you weren't in the aristocracy. You were going to public schools. You had enough money. The aristocrats were those who went to the top public schools Eton, Harrow, Winchester, and always ended up at Oxford and Cambridge. It was they who ran the country.

My dad's second wife, June, came from aristocracy; she was part of the Westmoreland family. There's a whole spine of those families that are not necessarily lords and ladies anymore, but they're spin-offs from that class, and they do certain things that other people don't.

That's what's so pernicious about English society: it is so graded.

Years later, in 1978, when I was rehearsing *The Coyotes* in Salmon Arm, BC, with the Caravan Stage Company, my dad phoned me up from London:

"Will you ever forgive me?" Never had my dad asked for forgiveness before. I said, "What's the matter?"

He said, "I'm going to become a Lord." Long silence. "What?!"

Lords appointed by the government (rather than inheriting the title) are "Life Peers." That's what Jeremy was to become. Until the appointed "Life Peers" started to build up to a proper number, the House of Lords was made up exclusively of the aristocracy, plain and simple. They would not be part of the House of Commons; they would be part of the House of Lords. And when you go into the House of Lords, you know you're in the House of Lords: "Good morning, Your Lordship. How is Your Lordship today? Does Your Lordship need anything?" And they make a couple of hundred a day. You go into this chamber that is red and gold and ermine and blah-blah-blah, and if you're a son of a Lord, like I was when I went in with my dad just once, you have the option of sitting at the feet of the speaker of the House of Lords. I preferred to sit with the wives. After the war, Jeremy ran as a Labour candidate in the election that led to the first Labour Party majority government; he remained a Labour Party member until he joined the Social Democrats, who split with the party hardline. He and I had come to serious blows over the events of the late sixties because he was fiercely against revolutionary tactics, direct action, and anything illegal. He thought revolutionary actions led to unhappiness and tyranny. His reading of history is probably quite right. We had major disagreements, usually fostered by my dear grandmother, Mary Hutchinson, who liked to stir things up.

The first of my lessons in class-consciousness, then, was from Len Hutton, and the second came at one of our family Sunday lunches when the conversation turned to the scathing reviews of Beckett's *Waiting for Godot*, directed by a very young Peter Hall, which had just opened at the Arts Theatre Club. We are in 1955, and my grandmother, Mary, has joined us for lunch. We all know that she has a very strong relationship with Samuel Beckett.

"What is this new play?" My dad loves to take digs at his mother. He has a wicked sarcasm, sometimes unpleasant. He and my mum start to get on a riff of:

"What's this play about?"

"What's it all for? 'Going nowhere, doing nothing?'" "Who is this Godot fellow?"

Mary rises to her full five foot two. "YOU ARE ALL SO BOURGEOIS!"

And she turns on her heels, slams the door, slams the front door . . . and that is that for a few days. Nine-year-old me wonders, "What does bourgeois mean? Can you tell me what bourgeois means?"

"Bourgeois" has remained a sort of wonderfully difficult thing to articulate and define. Mary, in many ways, was the ultimate bourgeoise. I had to ponder that.

Drawing of Mary Hutchinson by Henri Matisse, 1936

Sailing the "Kate" in Chichester Harbour

CHAPTER 2

Growing Up

On the basis of playing my guitar to the New Zealand sheep for the brilliant Mr. Code, I won a small bursary which allowed me to go to Bryanston. Nowadays, it's one of the smartest of the smart schools, but in those days, it was considered a progressive but less distinguished version of Gordonstoun, the school that Prince Charles attended.

Bryanston was more or less modelled on Gordonstoun, with perhaps a less disciplinary attitude and a more liberal outlook; nevertheless, you were subjected to cold baths or showers first thing in the morning, with a prefect checking you off, and an early morning walk before breakfast. To all us young newcomers these things were a bit astonishing.

When you first arrived you didn't go into the main, extraordinary, red-brick, horror-story-of-the-Victorian-attempt-to-look-eighteenth-century massive house with two wings and a great rotunda that you drive around—you were placed in a junior house, some distance from the main building. There were two junior houses and mine was called Durweston House. We were with about thirty boys, and we biked the one and a half miles to school because it was too far to walk. When you arrived at the big school, you went to below stairs to the lockers and tuck room. You had a tuck box—which hopefully your family had filled with all your favourite things, and which emptied very fast. Then you went into a little chapel down in the basement for prayers, and then you emerged up into the traffic of the rest of the school.

The big event in my first term was when we were all heralded to attend prayers upstairs in the big assembly room, and off we trooped. As we went, there were senior boys whispering, "Don't sing after the first line of the hymn." Up we go into the full assembly. I think it was none other than the Blake's "Jerusalem," a very rousing, beautiful hymn:

"And did those feet in ancient times walk upon England's pastures green . . ."

Everybody started to sing and at the end of the second line, eighty percent of the school stopped. All the masters were singing away as loud as they could, with just a few of the prefects joining in. The shock of this insubordination registered on the faces of most of the staff and was palpable. We were delighted by having pulled off a protest. It was a tremendous instruction in direct action: the power of revolt. We didn't really know what the revolt was.

The new headmaster was Mr. Fisher, who was not nearly as attractive and eloquent as his predecessor, Mr. Code, and had much less of a sense of humour. Mr. Fisher stepped to the lectern to say, "Cases of beer and wine have been discovered under the studies floorboards of half a dozen or more of the top prefects of the school, and this is not to be tolerated ever. I have expelled . . ." And then he read out the list of those who he'd expelled. That's when we realized why we hadn't sung.

Later, when I considered the event, I thought, *Our action was a protest, no more than that. We registered our disapproval, much like the Campaign for Nuclear Disarmament* (which at the time was gathering steam with the famous Aldermaston March) *registered serious opposition to Nuclear Armament, but had no real impact other than protest.* But this was the early sixties, and protest was the name of the game and a prelude to the much more radical movements of the late sixties and early seventies.

For some bizarre reason—mainly, I suppose, because of my dad and his wartime experience in the Navy—I joined the Sea Cadets. You had to do some extracurricular activity: you were either in the Sea Cadets or you were in the Pioneers. The Pioneers, the proud invention of Bryanston, put the school to work on good projects. Among other things, they built a genuinely beautiful Greek theatre. The work of the Sea Cadets was *drill.* And it wasn't long before we had a drill out front on the rotunda, where we had to line up and stand to attention, still as a post. After five minutes or so I began to wobble; I had never experienced standing at attention this long. I realized this was not for Nick. I'm not sure if I actually fell over, but, feeling deeply ashamed, I left the drill. As I was sitting dejectedly down in the basement on my tuck box, a group of slightly older boys, who were connected in various ways with my family, came to commiserate. One of them was Larry Boulting, who became a great friend:

"Hey, you know, really, you're one of us, aren't you? Right? Let's go for a smoke."

So off we went to "quickie" number one, amidst the bushes surrounding the school, and puffed away . . . that was the start of my smoking.

I didn't adjust well to the fact that we were thrown out of bed at seven o'clock in the morning and had to line up in shivering England cold in the corridor and then go and dip into a cold bath. How cold was up to the prefect who was monitoring us. And we had to jump in the tub, get all the way under, and come out shivering even more than before. That was pretty brutal. Later on, it was just a cold shower. But there was a period of time, in the seventies particularly, travelling on the Caravan, that if I ever had the opportunity to dive into cold water first thing in the morning, I would. If the sea or a river was at hand today,

I would probably still do it. I might wait till after coffee. But it does have an invigorating and awakening impact.

Our punishment was to run. If your shoes weren't up to snuff or for some other trivial fault, you got a *morning run* which took away your break at eleven o'clock. If you did anything more serious, you had an *afternoon run*, a long-distance run. You didn't necessarily have to run the whole thing. You could walk some of the way and converse with all your criminal gang who were on the run too. So, it was a gentle punishment and that's all there was. Well, that and expulsion.

I was lucky that when I finished my first year and graduated from Durweston House, I was put in Portman House which was run by our housemaster and extraordinary history teacher Mr. Royds, who had been tutor to King Haile Selassie of Ethiopia. He was the genuine article—a wise and good teacher. He could be tough and send me to bed crying, but he would also be available to talk to, and he was known to let his charges have the odd cigarette in his study. He gave me the love of history.

In my first year, I read a play or two for our play-reading club. I wasn't particularly turned on by that. In the second year, I was drafted to do a play for the house drama festival. I chose N. F. Simpson's *The Hole*, which is a hilarious play: there's a hole in the road, and there's no reason for it, and these absurd characters come and talk about it. That was quite good fun. I suppose that was where my enthusiasm for theatre began to develop. Shortly thereafter, some of the smoking crew and I organized a pocket theatre in the Portman House attic where we would do nothing but modern works.

I started my real directing career the next year with Ionesco's *Jacques ou la soumission* for a house drama festival. John Blatchley, who at the time was the director of the Central School of Speech and Drama in north London (the school my mum and Lawrence Olivier had attended together many years before), agreed to adjudicate our festival. (I don't remember whether it was me who managed to get him or my mum or somebody else.) He had been one of Michel St Denis' prominent students and had a gentle humourous, engaging, sharp-witted manner that galvanized everybody's enthusiasm and understanding of their roles, because we finally got some serious criticism:

"Nick, why were your shoes so dirty?!"

I mumbled an incoherent reply.

"It's all about details, Nick." From then on, I became serious about directing.

Up until that point in my life, I had been plagued by pinches on the cheek, and, "Is he going into the theatre like his mummy?" Not to mention the weight of unspoken family tradition suggesting I might end up as a barrister. The possibility of becoming a director, as opposed to an actor, gave me an "out" from following in my mother's footsteps.

Going into that fourteen-year-old summer, Larry Boulting (who had become a real friend following my drill debacle) and I decided to go on a Spanish expedition. We had been reading Laurie Lee and George Orwell's accounts of the Spanish Civil War, and we were totally fixated on Spain.

Laurie Lee was a very special person in my life, a friend of my parents. When he came to dinner with his beautiful wife Katalina, he would bring his guitar and sing all sorts of folk songs. It was because of him that I decided to learn guitar despite my parents' protestations, who thought I should start with the piano. I overcame their resistance with a compromise that first I would learn classical guitar.

Larry and I persuaded our parents, who miraculously agreed to the Spanish expedition. We took a train from the south of France to Barcelona. And then we made our way in buses. The fascists had won the civil war, and we were in fascist Spain with fascist policemen. I never really noticed it being terribly fascist. On our way south, we stopped in this little place called Lorca—a very, very poor town where some people were living in troglodyte caves. I had never seen poverty like this: children with bloated bellies and girls with old women's faces. We always had kids running after us, asking us for money. I climbed a rocky hill, and as I went by the ruins of a church, I heard these cries and screams and found a woman lying in the rubble, trying to give birth. I was thunderstruck. Of course I had never been anywhere near a birthing and had no idea what I should do. I finally came to the conclusion that she had, apparently, chosen this spot and I would do best to leave well alone. Lorca—the town, the starving kids, the woman giving birth in the church's rubble, the caves—had a profound effect on the fourteen-year-old boy who had never experienced such abject poverty.

And then on to Granada in Andalusia. And just like everywhere, there would be a group of young boys who would surround and befriend us, and we would buy them Coca-Cola while we drank wine. Coca-Cola was twelve pesetas and wine was one peseta. And they would take us to the sights, to flamenco performances and bullfights. We saw a few bullfights, repulsive and beautiful. Beautiful in the pageantry and elegant skill of the matadors, repulsive in the cruelty of the picadors, astride their mattressed horses, as they stuck their lances remorselessly into the bleeding bull to anger and weaken it. And then the final thing, which built over a number of days—a trip to the red-light district to lose our virginities. The boys from the town all claimed their dads had taken them. I'm not sure they had. They were our age.

We would knock at the dimly lit doors, then get the giggles and run off, then knock at another dimly lit door and get the giggles and run off again. Finally, we knocked at one and held our breath and it opened onto a long corridor. Right at the end was La Mama—the black, hairy, classic, middle-aged, thick-legged, red-skirt-tight-round-those-massive-limbs Mama. "This isn't what we came for!" We were sat down and given drinks and, leaning over us, she crawled up our legs with her fingers going, *"Quieres fucky fucky fucky?"* It was a nightmare. I pretended that I knew no Spanish, but Larry the translator went, *"Ah no, yo poquito mal a l'estomaco."* So, Alka-Seltzer was sent for and Alka-Seltzer came, and we looked at each other and bolted. That was it. We didn't do it. What a letdown. It took the sheen off our journey, so that by the time we got to Malaga, we were arguing. I then went to Gibraltar and caught a plane home.

Larry was the son of one of the Boulting brothers—major British filmmakers in the fifties and early sixties. His path was film. During the next terms at school, we developed a scenario based on Louis MacNiece's poem "Eclogue from Iceland." The poem came out of MacNiece's trip to Iceland with his lover, W. H. Auden, and contained discussions between them and epiphanies about the old god Thor.

And so, four of us packed up our bags and went to Yorkshire, where we scouted out a basic location on one side of the river. Every day we waded across, carrying the sixteen-millimetre camera to this cave where we filmed the discussions. Every night we'd go to the pub and get stinko-drunk and collapse on the way home in a barn where there was extremely itchy straw. My whole face got inflamed from it.

We would take off to the moors to shoot the scenes with the god. We went through all the things that always happen when four boys go on a long adventure—getting on each other's nerves, getting depressed, getting stinko-drunk—but we did come back with footage in the can.

We went to Stepleton with a projector and a tape recorder and tried, unsuccessfully, to dub it. That was the end of our movie, *Eclogue from Iceland*. Somewhere the footage waits in the can.

Peggy and I were visiting Michel St. Denis in his little house just outside of Paris, and in the course of a conversation about what to do after school, he suggested I go to Strasbourg to audit rehearsals of Pierre Lefèvre's upcoming production of *The Good Woman of Szechuan*.

Which is what I ended up doing—improving my French and watching Brecht in French going through all the stages of rehearsal. I became part of a little after-hours quartet of young actors from the show. Of course, I was unrequitedly in love with the girl, and the lead actor was unrequitedly in love with me, and the fourth member of the quartet was Alain, who became a great friend.

I was beginning to consider my options once school finished for good. My plan at the time had been to take a year off. I'd go and audition for Blatchley at the Central School of Speech and Drama because I thought I should learn to act before I did anything else. But when I came back from the summer at Strasbourg, I thought maybe I should apply to the stage management and directing program there, instead. I mean, look at Peter Brook, Peter Hall, John Barton, Trevor Nunn. These were the great directors of the day, and they barely ever acted. You can be a director without being an actor. This has always been a permanent argument within myself, but looking back, I have to admit that acting contributed hugely to my skill as a director.

One of our final productions in our pocket theatre was Pinter's *The Caretaker*. I got to play Aston, which marked me forever, because he has this long, long, speech—the longest that I'd ever learned—about losing it and going to the psychiatric hospital and getting electric shocks. And thus I learned what electric-shock therapy could be from the inside. I relived the speech every time I sailed close to the electroshock therapy wind in psychiatric institutions later on in life.

Reading the speech over today, I think what a hefty load on a fifteen-year-old. Here is an extract:

"They asked me questions, in there. Got me in and asked me all sort of questions.

Then one day . . . this man . . . this doctor I suppose . . . the head one. He called in. He said I had something . . . some complaint . . . We've decided, he said, that . . . in your interests, there's only one course we can take. He said . . . but I can't exactly remember . . . how he put it . . . he said we 're going to do something to your brain . . . Well they were coming round to me, and the night they came I got up and stood against the wall.

They told me to get on the bed, and I knew they had to get me on the bed because if they did it while I was standing up they might break my spine, so I stood up and then one or two of them came for me, well I was younger then, I laid one of them out, and I had another one round the throat, and then suddenly this chief had these pincers on my skull and I knew he wasn't supposed to do it while I was standing up, that's why . . . anyway he did it.

I've often thought of going back and trying to find the man who did that to me."

The other remarkable thing that made life at school almost bearable was that our gang had discovered this old shack, where the keeper of the hounds would once have stayed when any of his foxhounds were being quarantined. It was isolated from everywhere and was a half-hour walk over the hills and far away. A place to let off steam. We furnished it with junk from the second-hand stores in our local town. And we had a wind-up record player, wine, and food. We'd invite girls over from our sister school, Wardour Castle. It was a magical place that began my pull away from the most civilized aspects of my over-civilised life. I loved that.

My other escape was Stepleton House, the grand one that the Robinson family acquired. Peggy would come for visits, by which time the Robinson's lifestyle, which had been supported by at least a dozen servants, was dwindling in true Chekhovian fashion. The servants didn't want to be servants anymore. The economy had shifted. It became more and more stressful to run the house, the garden, and the estate. By now there was normally, maybe, a cook and one butler. Once, when I went over to see Peggy, the cook had just quit, so I said, "I'll cook dinner."

There were steaks. Oh, good—I can cook steaks because my sister in France has taught me how. I go into a vast kitchen, I get the steaks out of the fridge, and they're big steaks, and I bash them around a bit to flatten them. I cook them up and serve them. Everybody has a good old time chewing.

"But they're very good, Nick, very good steaks."

And then the butler comes into the dining room, and he whispers to Mrs. Robinson and she bursts into laughter.

"Well," she says, "you'll never guess what? The butler just found all the steaks in the fridge when he was looking for the dogfood."

I had cooked the dogfood for the people and got major colours for it.

The culmination of these years of theatre exploration was a production of *Hamlet,* staged in the Bryanston Greek theatre and involving almost all my theatre buddies, with the added benefit of girls from our "sister school" playing the women's parts. Mr. Fisher, who had remained very unpopular since the hymn-singing event in my first year, proved to be passionate about the theatre and quite a good director. My current way of introducing my good friends Alan Moses and Jonathan Keats is that they played Rosencrantz and Guildenstern to my Horatio. There was much romance in the air and almost love affairs. Hardly surprising—we were sixteen and seventeen.

Then, finally, the agonizing week of A-level exams. I did pass them all . . . just . . . and was therefore eligible for Oxford (my father's secret wish), but the exams had convinced me that essays were not to be part of my future. And I determined to apply to the École du Centre Dramatique de l'Est in Strasbourg.

And I got in. The first term was a combination of massive culture shock, bringing my French up to an operational level, at sea with all the French theatre terminology, but delighting in the camaraderie of the students, the brilliance of the teachers, and above all, the food and wine. Pierre Lefèvre had taken me under his wing. I followed, as his assistant, his renowned mask work with the first-and second-year actors. Hubert Gignoux, the artistic director of the theatre, came back from Poland and gave us an amazing description of the work of Grotowski's Physical Theatre, which would have a huge impact on theatre to come. But the most important thing was that, with much difficulty, I lost my virginity.

At the end of the first year, Peggy came out and we drove off to the south of France. It was on the road that she dropped the bombshell that she was going to divorce Jeremy. There had been signs for quite a while, but I had never pursued them. But I knew that one reason for going to Bryanston was to get away from home, which wasn't a happy place. The news was shattering, and my first reaction was anger that, in order to protect us, they hadn't told me and my sister what was going on. It's the age-old dilemma of parents—protection versus truth. Jeremy had been having a serious affair for four years. It looked to me, at the time, like he was the guilty party.

The other memorable moment of our trip together was visiting the great director and visionary Gordon Craig in his house in Vence. What an extraordinary character. He was in his nineties, clad in a white coat, with streaks of white hair going in all directions. At the top of our visit he appeared to dance in the street, though really that was just the intensity of his crazy energy. The rest of the visit was spent at his bedside, in non-stop conversation. I hadn't previously known a lot about Craig except for the books, magazines, and pictures bestowed on me by my grandmother Mary. Meeting him in the flesh drove me to discover more about his revolutionary ideas on theatre. He was dismantling naturalism and reinstating the mask. In fact, his magazine was called *The Mask*. He was refiguring the theatre without realism and realistic sets, and, of course, his one great production was *Hamlet* in Moscow for Stanislavsky and the Moscow Arts Theatre.

Back at the school for my second year, much improved in French and with much more confidence, I continued the mask work with Pierre Lefèvre and directed a student production of *The Duchess of Malfi*. At the end of the second term, I was offered a house-sitting gig in the south of France. An absolutely beautiful stuccoed "maison du midi" perched above Cannes, walking distance from the classic "village du midi". I found a solitary rhythm never before experienced—writing, reading, cooking, eating, and sleeping. But as the weeks wore on, I got lonely. I read Thomas Mann's *Magic Mountain*. And, after diving too deeply into a river, developed serious sinusitis, which I related to the hero of *Magic Mountain*—his suffering and flights of imagination. I was rescued from my loneliness by my sister Eliza who came to visit from Paris, where she lived. It was a very special time for us, for only recently had we begun to appreciate each other; we were closing the five-year age gap and had both managed to deal, more or less, with the divorce of our parents. Eliza had moved to Paris and found the classic tiny Parisian apartment in the Quatrième. She was getting work as a translator and developing her quite extraordinary talent as an artist.

One day, we went to a village fête where we met a charming couple—Jean-Louis (dark, handsome sculptor), and his younger wife (humorous, self-possessed, whip-smart Sylvianne)— who persuaded us to go and stay with them atop another *village perché*. They weren't exactly getting along. Jean-Louis' focus was Eliza, and Sylvianne's was me. And one fine siesta afternoon, as I drowsed on my little hideaway bed, Sylvianne, throwing caution to the wind, led us to a steamy "love in the afternoon." Jean-Louis' advances to Eliza were put off by the fact that she disclosed to him that she was pregnant, and eventually he generously took her to Marseilles for the termination. Eliza told me all of this later; I was completely unaware of her situation at the time. A number of months later, a little more than nine to be exact, I received a letter from Sylvianne, informing me that she had given birth to a son and she was ninety-five percent sure he was mine. Stéphane. What did I make of that? Paternity was not something that I had yet considered. What's more, Eliza's hidden pregnancy and abortion was quite upsetting, after what I had thought was our new-found intimacy. Those few days with Jean Louis and Sylvianne had revealed a whole new raft of life's complexities.

My first task in the third year at Strasbourg was as assistant to Pierre's production of O'Casey's *The Bishop's Bonfire*. There was a lovely gal who was playing the ingénue, and a group from the cast went off to the bar on a Friday night to consume a large amount of alcohol. This was normal practice in Strasbourg, whether at noon or night. But more so on a Friday night.

We staggered out of the bar. I had my little blue Mini parked outside, and I was getting in, when this lovely girl jumped on the roof, and I thought, *Oh well, what do we do now?* So, I pulled out and set off down the road, followed by the other guys in their Quatrelle. We were getting up speed as we went through town and hit the Place de la Republique, a great big, long circle. Our friends in the Quatrelle were close behind and she was having great fun on the roof, so, to

Sylvianne Cantin

my everlasting shame, I put my foot down to zoom around the circle. Disaster happened. While I watched in the mirror, she spiralled off the roof, hit the curb, and broke her ankle. Shame flooded over me and remained at high tide for quite a while.

The worst thing, apart from the awful feeling I had while getting her treated, was having to confess to Pierre what I had done to his leading lady. Pierre was visibly upset but gentle in his reproach. Even worse than that, I had to appear before Hubert Gignoux, who was much tougher. But there were no further consequences. I guess they thought I'd had punishment enough: shame. It endures to this day in the top five of my most shameful deeds.

My dear grandmother Mary, in her late seventies and early eighties, would disappear every month or so. The family would make up great jokes around the theme of "What's she up to now?" She would take the train from Victoria to New Haven and then the ferry to Dieppe and then the train to Paris, and she would stay at my aunt's apartment in Rue de Grenelle. She went because she was absolutely passionate about Sam Beckett and was a great friend of his. She was always a great ear to great writers, as she had been earlier with T. S. Eliot when he was struggling with his masterpieces. I came to Paris when my grandmother asked Sam Beckett to tea, and I was invited—a great privilege, as no one in the family had ever been in his presence before. Later, Peggy got to know Sam quite well when she did *Happy Days* at the National Theatre. The thought of meeting him, though a great privilege, was nerve-wracking. But when he arrived there were no nerves at all, because he was absolutely easy-going and a real listener. He lay, sprawled, with his long legs crossed on the big double bed—in no way the stern, imposing image that I'd imagined. My grandmother, as always, perched on her chair like a bird. And we had tea.

The high point of my third year was stage-managing a touring production of *Montserrat,* part of the professional company's touring season. It was a serious responsibility and I got to wield the magical *baton du regisseur,* the stage manager's staff, that was pounded on the stage floor, and whose nine swiftly repeated knocks were followed by three portentous knocks that cued the curtain. I was also walking on as a Spanish soldier, hair dyed black and what today would be called out as "brown face."

But the most enjoyable part of this two-month tour, which went to small towns and villages from Alsace-Lorraine to Burgundy and Switzerland, was the food. An older member of the cast would know the best places to go, and our midday meal was almost always indescribably delicious. The evenings after the show comprised three to four to five hours of poker for high stakes.

You gotta know when to hold 'em
Know when to fold 'em
Know when to walk away
Know when to run
You never count your winnings
When you're sitting at the table
There'll be time enough to count 'em
When the dealing's done.

- Kenny Rogers, "The Gambler"

A major life lesson that I had yet to learn.

When I did Dürenmatt's *The Physicists* with Gignoux, as his assistant, he directed in the traditional French method, with everything pre-ordained in what would become the prompt book for the show—every move diagrammatically ordained and analytically justified. I had learned the system throughout my training but was beginning to question it. I pondered the contradictions between his process and the inspiring account he had given us following his visit to Grotowsky's Poor Theatre and I was learning the magic of improvisation from Pierre's mask work.

During my third year, I met my first Québécoise, Marie-Claire Nolin, a first year acting student at the school. She was unlike all those French women that I'd courted or bedded because she was a full-on Québécoise—sharp, feisty, and slightly crazy—and we had a lovely fling. She introduced me to marijuana and Bob Dylan. Up to then, I was just singing Georges Brassens, Jacques Brel, and other French songs. Rock and roll was new to me, and I couldn't figure it out on my classical guitar. It just didn't work. But Bob Dylan. Wow! A few years later, it was Marie-Claire who'd be one of the Québécoises who brought me to Montreal.

I didn't know what the next thing for me would be, but then I got a letter from Peggy saying, "Peter Hall is thinking about whether you'd like to be assistant director at the Royal Shakespeare Company in the coming season? What do you think?" Well, what *did* I think? It was an amazing offer, but nevertheless it gave me serious pause. I had always struggled with the privilege of being Peggy Ashcroft's son. Three years in France had spared me this burden, and now this offer from Peter smacked of nepotism. On the other hand, to work alongside Peter Hall, John Barton, Trevor Nunn, and Clifford Williams, not to mention the extraordinary company of actors that had developed with the Royal Shakespeare Company, wasn't something you could dismiss lightly.

So, I went with some hesitation. I didn't know anything about English theatre practice— you know, the little things: when do you have coffee and what is *blocking*? At the same time, I was going back to this very familiar space. Stratford, the theatre, my past. I'd spent lots of time in Stratford. I knew the stage. I knew The Dirty Duck, the actors'pub.

I was unaware at the time that English theatre was in the middle of its second golden age. The Royal Court Theatre, under my godfather George Devine, had exploded into a whole new movement of contemporary plays from John Osborne's *Look Back in Anger* to Wesker's *The Kitchen* and Edward Bond's

Saved. The repertoire was radical and challenged the Lord Chamberlain's iron-grip on censorship.

Hard to believe that up until the mid 1960s, the Lord Chamberlain had to approve every play or performance and/or apply censorship removing scenes or speeches. Joan Littlewood (*Oh! What a Lovely War*), a visionary of working class theatre, was running Stratford East, mixing music and theatre in a way that was entirely original at the time. The Royal Shakespeare Company, which was born out of the old Stratford Memorial Theatre, had been transformed by Peter Hall, who brought Peter Brook, Michel St. Denis, and Peggy together as artistic directors, and who forged a permanent company, really the first of its kind, that would perform Shakespeare at Stratford and new works in London during the winter season.

At Stratford, the epic *Wars of the Roses*, Shakespeare's *Henry VI*s and *Richard III*, was condensed by John Barton into three plays, and on certain days all three plays would be performed—a completely new idea. In London, at the Aldwych, which became the RSC London home, Peter Brook blew everybody's minds with his productions of *King Lear, Marat/Sade*, and a collective-creation, *US*, whose subject was the Vietnam war and us. Again, the idea of a collective creation with a company was a relatively new practice in the theatre and completely new for me and inspiring. The first half was the horror story of the Vietnam War, and the second half was how that affected us. At the very end was an unforgettably poignant moment. Following the maelstrom of war, there was a moment of total silence and an empty stage onto which walked, one by one, every single member of the cast—so, "Oh, we're going to a curtain call." And they're all lined up in front of us, looking at us. There's a moment of total suspension . . . and then a man in a suit comes on with a box on a little table. And he goes to the middle of the stage and faces the audience for maybe two or three minutes in absolute silence. And then the man opens the box, and the lid opens towards the audience, so you can't see what's in it. He puts his hand in the box and he picks something out and casts it towards the audience. And it's a butterfly. It took my breath away. And this butterfly flies towards the light. Then he picks another one out of the box and throws it and now there are two butterflies. And then three butterflies, and that's it. And nothing happens. And some people go, "Oh, God," and stomp out. And everybody else just sits there in silence for what seems like twenty minutes. I have never sat in a theatre before in total silence—moved, inspired, shocked, endeavouring to make sense of what has just occurred and how it relates to the Vietnam War. The remaining audience members trickled out in their own time.

So, I arrived in Stratford in the thick of all that—a French-theatre-trained twenty-year-old novice. My first assignment was to assist John Barton, Clifford

Williams, and Trevor Nunn in remounting the second trilogy of *the Wars of the Roses* -the *Henry IV*s and *Henry V* . What I remember most were the notes sessions. Three loquacious directors giving notes to a cast of thirty until five o'clock in the morning—it was Equity Union rules to the winds. But the notes were fascinating, inspiring, and taught me their importance as a fundamental directing tool.

Rehearsals could get so intense. I remember one day, John Barton sitting at the director's table in the stalls. He had one cigarette going, and then he put it behind his ear, and lit another one, and suddenly he had three cigarettes in his mouth, and the stage manager said, "John?!" And John fell over the back of his chair, to much laughter.

The next assignment was assisting Clifford Williams' production of *Twelfth Night*—not a particularly brilliant one, but great fun. Watching the whole process revealed what a great play Twelfth Night is. Outside of the theatre, my six months at Stratford was taken up with village cricket with the company team, where I made great friends with Trevor Nunn, who was closer to my age, and a lot of beer was drunk.

Theatre Toronto

presents

LITTLE MURDERS

by JULES FEIFFER

ROYAL ALEXANDRA THEATRE—FEBRUARY 7-25, 1968

LITTLE MURDERS
by JULES FEIFFER

CAST
In Order of Appearance

Marjorie Newquist	AMELIA HALL
Kenny Newquist	RICHARD MONETTE
Carol Newquist	ERIC HOUSE
Patsy Newquist	MAUREEN FITZGERALD
Alfred Chamberlain	COLIN FOX
Wedding Guests	JANET AMOS, DAPHNE GIBSON, BARBARA HAMILTON, DAVID HEMBLEN, E. M. MARGOLESE, JACK O'REILLY, TERRY TWEED
Judge Stern	HUGH WEBSTER
Reverend Dupas	JOSEPH SHAW
Lieutenant Practice	GERARD PARKES

The Action of the play takes place in the Newquist apartment. The time is the present.

ACT 1—February

ACT 11
Scene 1: One Month Later
Scene 2: Two Months Later
Scene 3: Four Hours Later

ACT 111—Six Months Later

Production by NICHOLAS HUTCHINSON
Designed by RALPH KOLTAI
Costumes by REG SAMUEL
Stage Manager KENNETH FRANKEL
Assistant Stage Manager PETER HAWKINS

*THERE WILL BE TWO INTERMISSIONS OF 10 MINUTES

CHAPTER 3

Toronto

A few months later I walked into the Old Vic, where Clifford Williams, for whom I had been an assistant director at Stratford, was rehearsing, and he said:

"Hey Nick. Wanna go to Toronto?"

"Where's that? Oh, sure." I didn't have anything else happening.

"Well, you know, I'd really love you to come. I don't have any money. I can pay you a bit while we're there. But you'll have to make your own way there."

So, I boarded a Norwegian freighter in Bremerhaven and took off across the high seas to this unknown country from whose bourne no traveller returns. Stepping onto the ship, I asked a seaman where one could find a drink on board. With a very Norwegian accent he replied, "This ship is dry." The thought of two weeks on the high seas without a drop of alcohol was horrifying. But a few days later, as we cleared Ireland into the Atlantic, I was invited to a celebratory dinner with all the crew and regaled them with a few songs on my guitar, at which point the cook invited me to his cabin to drink. It was half schnapps and half Coca-Cola in large tumblers, and within four or five of those the floor was hitting me in the head, and I crawled, with great difficulty, back to my cabin. The worst of it was in the morning, with the inevitable hangover. The ship's engines had been turned off to fix its cooling system, and we were lolling in the ocean swell. But I had four scripts, and, as associate director, had to have decided which play I was going to direct by the time I got to Toronto. The one I couldn't do was Rolf Hochuth's scandalous play about Churchill, which Clifford was going to do. There was a farce that I couldn't stand. But I had seen *Little Murders* by Jules Feiffer—a New York satire on the theme of random urban shooting—and thought, "There's lots of grist in this mill." I was twenty. I was a little young.

Coming up the Saint Lawrence River . . . finally, it's smooth sailing after two weeks of ocean swell. On either bank, the maple trees are in full fall colour. It's enough to take your breath away. I'm excited with this new world, and Expo '67 is next. I've finally made it—late because of the ship's cooling system getting fixed—but I'm going to get off and go to Expo '67 in Montreal, which is in full swing, before I head up to Toronto. When I do get off the ship, I phone up and say:

"Hey, I finally got here. I'm gonna spend another day, okay? And then I'll be . . ."

"Oh, no, sorry. You've got to be in Toronto tomorrow for auditions."

"What?!" Auditions? I've never held auditions in my life. So on to the train I go. I get to Toronto:

"Where's Clifford?"

"Oh, they've all gone off for a couple of days to Expo 67."

"So how many . . . I'm seeing sixty people for the company? Don't we already have a company?"

"Yes. It's just a PR move."

So, I sit there while another middle-aged old woman does another Constance from *King John* that drives me around the fucking bend. And they all come in and every single one of them goes:

"Are you Clifford Williams?"

"No, I'm not Clifford Williams. I'm Nick. I'm the associate director."

That was the beginning of a pattern.

We had the Royal Alex Theatre for the season. It had recently been taken over by impresario extraordinare, Ed Mirvish, who had just restored it to its Victorian splendour—a twelve-hundred-seat auditorium with two balconies set close to the stage, giving a real sense of intimacy. It was an absolutely beautiful theatre. *Little Murders* was to be the second production, and meanwhile I was charged with setting up the Theatre Toronto Club, where I could do anything I wanted and be as experimental as possible, but I had to do three different performances every week. It was to build audience support. As a subscriber of Theatre Toronto, you could go to the shows at the Royal Alex and the Club.

The company was composed of many of the best professional actors in Toronto, who objected to a production group of . . . "fucking Anglo assholes who don't know anything about Canada." Being so young, cute, and having just turned twenty-one, I got off fairly lightly. I lived on the twenty-fourth floor of a tall apartment building in Rosedale with Mother Reg. Mother Reg was a much-loved head of wardrobe at the Royal Shakespeare Company. Brilliant and gifted at his job, he was full-on gay and gave great gay parties. This was well before the horrors of the AIDs epidemic. In Toronto the gay scene was emerging from the closet and there was a euphoric energy and sense of a movement that was gathering steam. This was all new to me as I awkwardly navigated the parties, but Mother Reg was always an understanding rock of support and good humour during my time in Toronto.

I do *Little Murders*. I actually go off and see the renowned author Jules Feiffer in New York. Feiffer is best known as one of the pre-eminent cartoonists of the time who managed his piercing social satires with irresistible humour.

His play *Little Murders* revolves around a New York Jewish family reacting to the ever-increasing gun violence that is outside, and by the end of the play they are madly firing out their high-rise window. I'm put on a train, and off I go and have a great get-together with Jules. He's an ultimately sympathetic man with no trace of condescension towards this young upstart, which is how I am frequently feeling at this time. I am so at sea. I've directed this and that. I've been an assistant in big houses, and I've done student productions, and I've done a couple of professional shows in smaller

houses, but I am so out of my depth. I'm still more confident in French theatre-speak than English and then add the Canadian element into the mix, absorb the unfamiliar New York reality of the play—all that while living on the giddy-making twenty-first floor of a high rise, having just turned twenty-one.

Designer Ralph Koltai's set for *Little Murders* was three enormous plexiglass panels upon which we projected images of urban warfare. It was pretty impressive. They brought the plexiglass panels into the theatre and put them up against a wall where there was a radiator. And they were very cold, so they all broke. My technical rehearsal was fucked. I had no tech at all. The lighting was guesswork, and after all that the actors all came on the stage to rehearse the curtain call . . . and that was more than I could handle. I had never actually done a curtain call, so I had to hand it off to Clifford. Clifford liked the show. And so, by and large, did the critics.

There's another part that is almost as dramatic. I was taken in hand by Clifford's extremely beautiful French wife, and we became lovers of sorts. It was very fraught, but I was at the peak of my randiness, if not the peak of my skill. Our trysts happened at their house when Clifford would be off at work, and we thought (or did we just hope) that he was completely unaware. The affair didn't last long, and we became good friends thereafter.

At the end of the season at Theatre Toronto, I'm called in for my end of term interview with Clifford. I'm wondering very much whether I would

Jules Feiffer standing behind the New York cast of Little Murders, 1967

like to stay on. It would be an affirmation. Or whether I would like to go. But do I want to? I have an offer in my pocket from Pierre Lefèvre from my old theatre school, the Centre Dramatique de l'Est in Strasbourg, to do a student production. And Clifford says:

"Nick, I always thought that you were one of those new Peter Brook kinds— you know, young and amazing—and . . . you aren't."

Which was a tad of a blow. I decided, well, okay, that's the way it goes. Never had I dreamed of being another Peter Brook, so in a way I could take the hit as a bit of a compliment. I hoped there was no personal revenge in the assessment. There was no question now my next move would be Strasbourg.

One of my roles throughout the season was to stand in for Clifford. I had once stood in for him at the auditions and then the day after my opening night of *Little Murders*, in a state of complete hangover and God knows what else, I had to fly to Ottawa as Clifford Williams' stand-in to address an international seminar on arts and culture that was being held in the beginnings of *The National Arts Centre*. It was half a building then. I had no idea what I was going to talk about. I tried to think of it in the plane, but I was really hungover. I got there, and there were all these erudites with their forty-page dissertations that they were delivering to the company assembled.

Eventually it came to my turn. Still not knowing what the heck I was going to say, I got up. And that was the first time I ever had to speak in public. I opened my mouth and started a sentence . . . at which point there's a voice behind me. The simultaneous translator is putting my unfinished sentence into French, which further confuses me, right? *What am I going to do?* And then, you know, as per usual, complete precipitous pressure forces you onwards. I tackled the work we were doing at the Theatre Toronto Club and miraculously the talk took off from there. It was very informal. People talked to me, asked questions, and it was a *va et viens*. That was my second stand-in.

For the third one, just after the Peter Brooke interview, I had to stand in for Clifford to be interviewed by a Québécois journalist, who turned out to be an absolutely strikingly gorgeous super-cool Québécoise. At the end of the dinner, she took me back to her hotel and we had what was probably the most exhilarating, breathtaking, and satisfactory night of love I had yet to experience. Who can explain the chemistry of making love? Certainly not I. But chemistry there was.

First thing in the morning, as I wrestle awake to go rehearse, she says, "Here, take this." She gave me a white pill, which I can only assume, after thinking about it, was probably Dexedrine. Which is a kind of upper. And off I went to rehearsal. It was revelatory. I was like, *I can do this, it's easy.* Up to this point, I didn't really know what I was doing as a director. Now it was clear, like knife through butter. Was it the sex? Was it the drug? Was it the liberation from having to be another Peter Brook? Who knows? But it set me up into a different space than I'd ever been in. I felt I could rely on what I had learned up to that point and trust myself.

Malvolio and Sir Toby (from William Shakespeare's 'Twelfth Night', Act II, Scene iii.
Painting by George Clint, 1770 – 1854

CHAPTER 4

Strasbourg

Pierre Lefèvre had invited me to direct his second-year students in *Twelfth Night*, a play I loved and for which I'd assisted Clifford Williams the year before. I knew the play and had a fascinating time exploring Shakespeare in French because there are many different translations. In *Twelfth Night*, the juxtaposition of verse and prose is finely tuned.

The standard French translation of the entire works of Shakespeare is by a nineteenth-century translator, Francois Victor Hugo, but he does them in prose—albeit elegant prose. However, we had a great family friend called Pierre Leyris, a poet and an ardent and serious translator of Shakespeare whose family I used to stay with as a child in Chambéry, in Haute Savoie. He had followed the verse/prose in his translations. To Leyris' slight chagrin, I opted to use Francois Victor Hugo in the prose and his translations in the verse. But it did accentuate the difference.

I had a lovely group of second year students, and among them was Véronique O'Leary, my Viola, with whom I fell in love. We started our rehearsal process, which was really fun, on the heels of my Dexedrine experience. For the drinking scene in *Twelfth Night*, we had an outrageous night where we turned off all the lights. I gave Toby Belch and Andrew Aguecheek two candles and two enormous bottles of red wine, and we had a hilarious rehearsal in the dark that illuminated the whole scene. For the first time, I felt a confidence in the work that was real.

We were having a really good time and then the rumbles began.

First from the student population in Paris. There were demonstrations, and then *paves* (cobblestones) got ripped up from the streets. The demonstrations increased and then the young workers joined the students on the barricades. The infamous French riot squad, CRS, responded with brutal *matraques* (batons) and tear gas. Then it started to spread to all the different towns. France has a well-earned reputation for taking their social issues into the streets—it's not for nothing that the French revolution gave rise to popular movements the world over—and this time the upheaval happened incredibly fast. And then, lo and behold, many of the factories in France were occupied by the workers. All of a sudden, back in Strasbourg, the entire Centre Dramatique de l'Est, the theatre school and the company, were on strike and the theatre was transformed into a permanent debating chamber where people just came and argued issues.

What started as a demonstration for student reform became more and more a *contestation* of the whole of society. President De Gaulle and the forces of the Right became the target. Interestingly enough, the basic ideology of the movement had originated amongst a small group at the University of Strasbourg about four or five years previously. They called themselves *Les situationistes,* and were inspired by the writings of Guy Debord and Raoul Vaneigem. Guy Debord's book *La societé du spectacle* was a serious, as well as a humorous, critique of consumerism and archaic communism.

A few years before, some of these *situationistes* had managed to take over the student union at Strasbourg and had published a pamphlet called *Misère en milieu étudiant.* It provoked the students of the university by confronting them with their subservience to the ideological conditions imposed upon them by the state, family, and the university system. They put the pamphlets on the seats at the opening events of the year at the university, and were met with absolute fury by the authorities. The students were kicked out, but a nerve was touched.

It was interesting, because Strasbourg is a very right-wing part of France. It's Alsatian, part German, part *indépendentiste.* There was a lot of support for De Gaulle and a lot of support for the extreme right. As a theatre, we're an island. But not completely because the university is full on. We meet day after day with our *comité de travailleurs* in the theatre with the students and the professionals. This is May '68. It's right in the midst of the troubles.

At first, the theatre students and I decided we had to go out and do something. We had to use our theatre skills. Our first project was a kind of guerrilla theatre. We dressed up as cops; we had *matraques* of rolled up newspapers and we tore into the university and played havoc. It was down and dirty, and fast but we managed to walk the line between provocation and humour. It was a bit naïve, but we did establish a serious connection with the students.

Then we decided we were going to work with the pamphlet *Misère en milieu étudiant* to make a *situationiste* show to be done in the university. We advertised that Europe #1, the pop radio station, was coming to Strasbourg to have a debate with the students and faculty over the current events. At this point, the situation was really serious because De Gaulle had disappeared and no one knew where he was. It was suspected that he might be in Germany, rallying his troops. Some people thought he might be on the point of resigning the presidency and that would herald a new day for the country. It was a very tense time. We advertised the radio show and set up a radio situation in the amphitheatre. We rehearsed about six *situationiste*-type ads about consumers, but otherwise we played the whole thing very straight. We had "speakers," whose names we invented, who got up and talked the right-wing line. And we had other people doing the other line.

After the first ad, people started wondering, *Wait . . . what?*

What's going on? They started to realise this isn't Europe #1. At which point our beloved artistic director, Hubert Gignoux, who had come to see how his students were doing, got up and very publicly left the hall in absolute, total disgust, which made us feel pretty good. It ended up with a raucous debate.

Then we introduced the Greek Messenger, who tears breathlessly into the auditorium. We asked him, "What's your news?" And he says, "I've come from Germany, and I've seen the 'Great One' [De Gaulle], but, *hélas*, like Marat in his bath, he is no more. *Qu'allez-vous faire de la France? Qu'allez-vous faire de la Patrie?*" (In reality, De Gaulle hadn't died in his bath but had in fact just slipped away to rally his crack troops, stationed in Germany.)

And that was how the real debate started with our audience of students. It was a debate about the future, the enormous implications of De Gaulle's departure for Germany, and where the movement was headed. For me, that was the beginning of agitprop theatre.

And there were no serious repercussions, other than we got a talking to from Hubert with all the things you'd expect someone in authority to say. Everyone else in the theatre was on board; Pierre Lefèvre was keeping a very low profile and said nothing. So there we were. About that time, the right wing responded; a day or two later, De Gaulle declared that he was returning with his crack troops from Germany, and would reassert order. He declared that general elections would be held and roused his support across the country. In Strasbourg, that support was huge.

A big demonstration of angry right-wingers came down and marched past our theatre, where we were cowering because we had the red and black flags out. Red for revolution, and black, the flag of anarchism They didn't care about a few actors and a pissy little theatre; they were headed to the university. The university was down a long boulevard and at the end of it was one of those classic eighteenth-century-really-nineteenth university buildings with the red flag flying on top. The demonstration advanced on it. There were lines of cops—the CRS, infamous for their brutality. They would be kept in their vans and given a lot of beer before being unloosed, then they'd go into the demonstrations with full force. The cops were positioned, blocking the demonstration's way into the university. Suddenly, the cops pulled out, and the demonstration went straight in at the university and started breaking the windows and forcing the doors. A couple of demonstrators got to the roof, lowered the red flag and raised the flag of France, the "tricolore." And then the guy who had raised up the red flag arrived to the edge of the roof. With his

Poster from the 1968, Sorbonne Silk Screen Studio

fist raised, he started singing, *"Allons, enfants de la Patrie, le jour de Gloire…"* ("The Marseillaise"), which is both the song of the French Revolution and the song of the right wing.

And so that was the end of *Twelfth Night*; it being May, term time had run out. At the heart of Shakespeare's play is the Lord of Misrule— how appropriate. My first version of the play coincided with May 68 in France, the second was going to happen two years later in Montreal during the "War Measures Act" and recently it occurred to me that the date of Twelfth Night is January 6(!) now infamous for the attack on the U.S. Congress and an ultimate expression of Misrule in its most negative form.

Within the space of, I suppose, only three or four weeks, almost everyone of my age was seeing life through a different lens. This was the world of "take your dreams for reality" on the big posters of the Sorbonne, where an amazing student-run silk-screen studio churned out beautiful designs of the revolution's demands. In Czechoslovakia, the revolution was in full force and about to be squashed by the Russian tanks; the anti-war movement in the US and the UK was in full cry, and you had students everywhere believing that there was another kind of reality worth fighting for. For me, the experience of those last few weeks had cemented an inkling I already had that the conventional professional theatre was no longer something I wanted to pursue.

For us students, because really, I was still a student: "What do we do? What is the mission now of the theatre?" We decided that we should attempt to form a company that would be based outside of any large city, if we could find some kind of rural place, some farm where we could get our act together.

Our search led us to Avignon, to the festival, to see how the Events were reflected in the theatre: "Well, let's see what's going on at the festival this year?" Right? And that was pretty exciting because we encountered the Living Theatre with *Paradise Now*, where the entire cast played naked for most of the play. There was alot of rolling and groping and stuff, which was pretty damned radical at the time. In as much as it challenged the norms of theatre, it inspired us; as for the actual content, we found it thoroughly decadent.

Having not yet found the rural venue for our company, most of us removed to Paris. My dad's sister, Barbara, had a flat in a lovely swanky part of the "Cinquième." Rue de Grenelle. I had a place where I could stay. We hung out in Paris as the movement gradually degenerated and dispersed and the streets were occupied by cops. For the first time, cameras came out and were placed in sensitive areas. You felt the unmistakable beginnings of repression. The Communist Party voted to hold the elections with De Gaulle. And so, there was no home for the revolutionaries anymore. The times were decadent: lots of drinking, lots of dope, lots of not knowing what we were doing.

It was at this time that Sylvianne wrote me to say she and Jean Louis would like to meet with me in Paris. Since the birth of our son Stéphane, I had done my best to keep in touch and whenever possible visit them in Le Broc, the same village where my sister and I had such an eventful visit two years before. I had even attended Stéphane's baptism, amongst Sylvianne's numerous family, who could not quite figure out who was this young Englishman accompanying her. Although by now Sylvianne and her husband Jean Louis had separated, he still played an active part in raising Stéphane and was assumed to be the father. We met up in a typical Parisian café, and the gist of a long discussion was that Jean Louis was ready to fully take on the paternity of Stéphane. I couldn't dispute the argument: Jean Louis was a steady presence even though he no longer lived with Sylvianne, whereas I was literally all over the place had no intention of settling down in Le Broc. Part of me was relieved—the pressure of paternity had haunted me. Sad in some ways that I would have to relinquish the fragile connection I had established with my son. But the die was cast, and we parted amicably—my only reservation was that from then on, we would be living a lie. Time would tell.

And then I met Michèle. Michèle was the girlfriend of Véronique's brother, Etienne, who was a very amazing *Nouvelle Vague* cinéaste and who was quite crazy, close to schizophrenic. She had been with Etienne for a long while, and I had been with Véronique, my lovely Viola: disarmingly pretty, the picture of innocence, disguising an acute intelligence and unshakeable commitment to the "cause," whatever that was at the time. She really was the ideal Viola. To stay with the *Twelfth Night* simile, Michèle was Olivia: older, elegant, darker, unconcerned with politics, who would eventually become a garden designer. Over the eating of a mango, droolingly evoking the eating scene from the movie *Tom Jones*, where Albert Finney and Diane Cilento lasciviously devour their meal, Michèle and I fell for each other.

"We're leaving our relationships and we're going to England." It was late summer of '68. We jumped in my Mini, went over at Dieppe, landed in New Haven, and went looking for my great friend Philip Trevelyan, who was shooting a movie out in Somerset. We arrived at a communal rural estate called Nettlecombe (where, ironically, scenes from *Tom Jones* had just been filmed). We stayed there and got our sea legs. After a while, our passion became somewhat worn and we were starting to have rows. It was coming to an end. It had been a quite an intense relationship—both of us having given up our respective O'Learys, leaving the French reality for an unknown English one— but despite everything, we developed a strong friendship that has lasted to this day.

I went back to London to see my mum. I headed immediately to the London School of Economics. This was the centre of the new leftist protests in London, where they were having similar meetings to the ones in Strasbourg, about what should happen, and which ideology should lead it. There were the Marxists, the Marxist-Leninists, the Trotskyists, the Maoists, the socialists, the anarchists, and everybody else, and also a quiet group sitting on the sidelines called Solidarity.

Almost immediately I was recruited by an American activist, Jim Caplan, who introduced me to the group of theorists—libertarian Marxists, who critiqued Lenin and Trotsky as having betrayed the working class by consolidating power in the party's central committee and eliminating the power of the workers' councils (Soviets) on which the revolution had been founded.

Demonstration in support of the Angry Brigade, 1969. Photo Steve Wood

CHAPTER 5

London to Montreal

And so I was recruited into that group by Jim. Jim was from Boston, cleaner cut than most of us—our hair was getting longer by the hour, whereas he cut an almost conventional figure. But our politics aligned, and it was that alignment that led us to Solidarity. In hindsight, I wonder about Jim—the movement was being infiltrated by all agencies English and American, and Jim did fit the profile, but he was a good friend, nevertheless. Almost simultaneously, and away from Solidarity, I got in with a couple of much more tousled, long-haired extremist fellows who wanted to really shake things up: "Solidarity wasn't going to do anything, the revolution was losing ground, and nobody was doing anything." I agreed with that . . . and they had really good hash.

We didn't have a name or anything like that because we were underground. There were probably about eight or nine of us. We started plotting direct actions on different targets, with sugar in gas tanks of vehicles belonging to government or business targets, and other rudimentary actions. Then along came a big demonstration in support of the Republican side of the Irish issue, in the face of the occupation by the English army in Belfast. I met up with our contingent, where wine bottles were being filled with gasoline and Tampax stuffed in the top for fuses. Off we went to the demonstration, with a few of them under our coats. In the middle of the demonstration a couple of our plucky guys tossed those into the Irish Consulate. It was the first fire-bombing that had ever happened in an English demonstration. The cavalry came, cops on horseback, marbles came out to fuck up the horses, and people were being banged about and trampled.

We finally peeled away from the demonstration as surreptitiously as we could and walked down Piccadilly to Green Park. We were all spread out so that we weren't a group, and as we got to the steps of the tube station, Jim and John, who had thrown the cocktails, were seized and taken off by a couple of Special Branch boys. We knew they must have seen us. So, I went to a call box and phoned my dad, Jeremy, the lawyer: "We need a lawyer, Father. Two of our guys got falsely arrested. They just picked on us."

To my astonishment, he actually did oblige. He got a wonderful lawyer from his chambers, who I still see to this day. He calls me his "witness." A very kind and humorous man, Robin. As I had a little "in" with the law, I became the organizer of our case, which was going to be at the Old Bailey in short order. I had to line up all the witnesses and prime them with what they were going to say. I skulked around the Old Bailey trying to avoid my father, as he did me.

I think we put up quite a good case. I mean it was all a bunch of lies. The police had no material evidence, so it was lies on all sides.

Anyway, we lost. Jim and John went down, so that was a bit of a loss, and we had to keep our heads down and deal with more social issues. For instance, we set up a people's justice committee, and I did quite a lot of work in Brixton, in the black area of London, trying to find defence for mainly black people in trouble with the law. In those days we had little respect for Law and Order. Ever since the Aldermaston marches for nuclear disarmament, the police in London and Paris were the enemy; Justice was Class Justice that protected private property and enforced laws that protected the interests of the ruling class. My dad and my grandfather were both barristers of note and believed passionately in the "rule of law," so I had absorbed much of that thinking growing up, but at the time of these events most of that had gone out the window.

At the same time, I was really having fun at a community centre at Kennington Oval on the South Bank of the Thames. I worked with a really good young group of non-actors on improvisation. It was the only thing I did that was vaguely related to theatre all this time. It was not brilliant, and it was a chore getting there, and I wasn't sure what I was doing, but it was kindling.

Meanwhile, the enthusiasm and gloss of the summer of '68 was disappearing in the face of pushback from the authorities. Our group now known as the Angry Brigade were determined to meet this pushback with pushback of their own. Reflecting the responses of our German and Italian counterparts, the Baader-Meinhof gang and the Red Brigades, we had connected with the Provisional IRA (the foremost group fighting the English army in Belfast). We started negotiations with them to obtain weapons. Of itself, this made me uncomfortable, along with the shadiness of our meetings and the by-now major paranoia about infiltrators. "Who was really who?" And, "Could you trust anybody in this situation?" We were starting to get into dynamite; all the aforementioned groups used it to target political and industrial adversaries, and since I was the only person with a car, I was moving all the dynamite. Frankly, it was awful looking stuff—leaky and threatening, sitting on the backseat of my car. I was getting even more uncomfortable.

I was living at Peggy's, at our old family house in Hampstead. One night we were having a big party at her place to celebrate the release of one of our guys from jail. We all dropped serious amounts of acid, got absolutely stupid, climbed out of the window of the study and started to climb far up the

sycamore tree. We weren't sure whether we could get down. So, the whole tree was full of loony tunes. The upstairs bedroom window flies open and Peggy, in her most formidable stage voice, booms, "What are you doing?!"

Hallucinogenically, we slither down the tree.

Peggy was very concerned about the group—also loyal to the core but with no idea what we were really up to. And Nan, my wee Scots nanny and now Peggy's housekeeper, an arch-Conservative, got to know everyone. She adored everyone. She would cook us breakfast when she could. But it was not a comfortable situation, and if I went to my grandmother's for dinner with my dad, my grandmother—the ultimate provocateur between my dad and me— would get us going to the point where I would leave the room, slamming the door. And Jeremy would be going, "I mean, honestly." Both my parents had an inkling of what we were up to, but not the full extent. My father, after all, had been indirectly involved with our trial at the Old Bailey, and Peggy had witnessed us in our most drug-crazed moment. I think they both sympathised with our ideals, and both dreaded the path we were on but staunchly refused to intervene.

In the spring of '69, I went back to Strasbourg to finish *Twelfth Night* because they were using it to showcase the graduation of the students I'd worked with the year before. So, I go back and reassert my friendship with Véronique. She's forgiven my dalliance with Michèle and there is still love, there always will be, but now we are just friends and comrades. We do a full-scale production of *Twelfth Night*; Véronique is an exquisite Viola, and although it fails to trigger a second May 68', it is a beautiful show. The greatest thing was that my grandmother Mary journeyed the whole way out to Strasbourg by train to see it. Not Dad, not Mum but my grandmother. She, of course, had been all the way with the revolution. She was the one saying, "Isn't this great, this revolution thing." She had a wonderfully romantic notion of revolution. But also, I think she realized how important the revolution was in the development of creative expression.

In the fall of '69, Véronique has returned to Québec, and I was back in England and increasingly uncomfortable in the Angry Brigade. One day the letter arrived. It's from Marie-Claire and Véronique, my closest friends from Strasbourg days, and they say, "We've got an anarchist theatre commune here in Montreal. And we need you."

Although it was a no-brainer, it was nevertheless a tussle because I would be forsaking my Angry Brigade comrades in their moment of most need.

Would I be a traitor to the cause? But do I really want to end up in Wormwood Scrubs with a long prison sentence? Do I want to be an agitator for the rest of my life? That's not who I am. I'm a theatre person.

I became a landed immigrant in Canada in 1970. Landing in Montreal was very different from arriving in Toronto in 1967. Like Paris and London, Montreal was in revolutionary foment, but the core of the movement was about independence of the French-speaking Québécois who had been colonised for centuries by the English. For a number of years, the *Front de Liberation du Québec*, a small radical group à la Angry Brigade, had been conducting intermittent actions (bombs in mailboxes etc.) and though they were considered a fringe group they nonetheless promoted the idea of Québec indépendence, a fundamentally popular demand. On the more legal front, René Lévesque, who eventually became premier of Québec, was beginning the Parti Québécois. There was a movement gathering steam.

The composition of our commune is half men, half women, half Francophone, half Anglophone, half Jewish, half Gentile, and if you shuffle us all into a deck of cards, there are three couples and me. We are rehearsing our first show, to be played on the picket line of workers striking against Québec pharmaceutical giant Squib for the right to unionise.

The commune is hungry. Marie-Claire and Véronique go and work at CBC, and I soldier off to the National Theatre School of Canada to try and get a job. The English section of the theatre school was run by William Davis, a Canadian actor best known for his role as "cigarette smoking man in *The X-Files*." He told me that the third-year students, who he was hoping I'd direct, had decided that they were leaving because they couldn't stand the school anymore and could I give it a go and see if I could persuade them to complete and graduate the school. So, of course, I had to give it a go and decided that I would try to sell *Drums in the Night* by Brecht. I found the students somewhat in disarray and fairly determined to leave, and did a hefty sell job, managing to convince the two most articulate members of the group, Michael Mawson and Sandy Nicholls—both destined to become celebrated theatre teachers. Finally, the group agreed.

We worked in a great empty space with stages here, there, and everywhere. *Drums in the Night* is all about the Spartakist uprising in Berlin in 1919, led by the revolutionary Rosa Luxembourg. In our production, a real pig's head came down from the ceiling during the bourgeois family's dinner as they gobbled it all up. Michael Mawson wrote some great music to Brecht's lyrics:

> *What can man do against a sea of fates?*
> *What can he do?*
> *Nothing*
> *There's lots of fish in the sea.*
> *What can he do?*
> *Learn to suffer without complaining.*

The students were very happy, and so was I, and I ended up falling in love with Sandy. What was different this time? For starters she was my first non-French amour, but really it was that we shared a close mutual understanding of life through the lens of theatre. She joined us in the commune. The commune had already written and performed the picket-line play for the squib workers. And now our second project—developing a show for the Montreal postal drivers who were on strike for better wages and working conditions, known as *Les gars de Lapalme*. I missed most of the work as I was still directing *Drums in the Night*, but the rest of the commune developed the play in a series of workshops. Sadly, the performance coming out of the workshops wasn't considered appropriate by the union leadership because the extreme proposals made in the show might jeopardise their negotiations. But it was, nevertheless, a very intense and exciting experience.

It was now summertime 1970. An unbearably hot, muggy, sweaty Montreal summer. In the fall, I was asked by the French section of The National Theatre School to direct a second year production of *Twelfth Night*. In almost the same way that my work with the second year students in Strasbourg had run up against the wall of May '68, we ran up and into the wall of October 1970, which was the vertiginous rise of the FLQ as a result of their kidnapping of the British Consul, James Cross, and eventually the Québecois minister, Pierre Laporte. I was the only person on staff at the school who talked with the students, met with them, talked about what was happening, and tried to give them information. In the first phase of the Cross kidnapping, the mood in Montreal was uncertain. But as it became clearer that the kidnappers knew what they were doing, and given that their demands often had a tinge of humour, they started to gain more and more popular support—to the point where Trudeau, the prime minister, was ready to negotiate. In those days,

Courtesy Canadian Press. Photo by Peter Bregg

governments were still finding their way as to how to deal with terrorists. Uppermost in their minds was avoiding harm to citizens rather than applying maximum repression on the perpetrators. One of the kidnappers' demands was for their manifesto to be read on CBC at prime time! It was very articulate, setting out independence for Québec under a basic self-managed socialist system. Going into the street the next day, it was impossible to miss the excited enthusiasm the manifesto had evoked. Then something terrible happened. Another group, completely unconnected with the Cross kidnappers, took a

Québec minister hostage, and their demands piled considerably more pressure on Trudeau. Trudeau responded by declaring Martial Law, investing Montreal with tanks and combat troops, and rounding up and jailing five hundred of the radical left.

So much of the struggle for a "Québec Libre" centred on making French the official language. By now I had managed to absorb enough Québécois to hold my own in discussions and debates. I was a bit of an oddity language-wise given my fundamental English, my adoptive French, and now my Québécois, which I loved. It was so much more direct and visceral than the hoity-toity snobbery of Parisian French. In fact, with the dramatic events unfolding, I was starting to identify as Québécois. Moving into the thick of the post kidnapping times, we left our apartment in the relatively genteel area near the National Theatre School and established the commune in a funky little flat in working class Saint-Henri—over the tracks from Westmount, the centre of the Anglo rich. A much starker reality and much more to our political taste.

January was a time of turmoil. It happened all over the United States, England, France, Italy, Germany, and everywhere else where there had been powerful popular movements. The governments responded with crackdowns, infiltration, and intimidation. In Québec and England there had been mass arrests of supposed terrorists or terrorist sympathisers; in the States the FBI conducted repression with the covert programme called COINTELPRO. This programme used five tactics: 1) Infiltration 2) Psychological Warfare 3) Legal Harassment 4) Illegal Force 5) Undermining Public Opinion. In Germany and Italy, the repression of the 1968 movement gave birth to the Red Brigades and the Baader-Meinhof gang. The question became, do you take up arms and have an armed uprising and push the envelope? Or do you try to work within the system? At the same time, the Feminist movement hit Montreal and hit our commune hard, which was already under a lot of stress. The women kicked the boys out of bed and out of the house, and we landed up on the street.

By which time, unbeknownst to me, my mind was starting to take off for the first time into hypomania edging on mania. This state is hard to describe, partly because, for the person afflicted, everything appears normal—maybe heightened to some degree, as it can appear under the effect of a strong dose of marijuana or a mild dose of LSD—until the mania gathers steam. And then one is inhabiting a totally different reality to the rest of the world. I found myself frequently wandering the city. Somehow, I got called into the National Theatre School and asked if I would take over the French section of the school as interim director. Perhaps the unexpected offer catapulted me further into this manic phase because we were revolutionary "*indépendentistes*," not pro-federal organizations represented by the likes of national theatres. But more than anything else, the idea that anybody other than a Québécois should be running things at this point in time, in the French section of the school, after the massive events of October, seemed ludicrous. I dreamed about it, wherever I was sleeping in whatever weird digs. And in my manic thinking, I was pondering what I could do to exploit the situation. Eventually I decided I would lay down a few conditions for taking the job. Off went I to the school, sat down with lovely Director General David Peacock, and said, "Well, you know, yes, I'll take the job, if you give me a passe-partout key right now and an office." (The key was to enable me to plunder material at the school.) And lo and behold, within half an hour, I had an office and a passe-partout key.

Things began to unwind. I started graffitiing the hallowed walls of the National Theatre School. Arriving at the main hall, there were two great big plants in front of the central courtroom, our theatre studio, just as Joy Coghill, the current director of the English section, came tripping down the stairs from her office. I grabbed a couple of branches of these extraordinary plants, ripped them off, tied them around her neck, and gave her a thumping kiss. I turned to see Jean-Pol Britte, the school's administrator, shaking in his shoes with disbelief and fury at the defamation of his sanctified place. I felt that blackening surge when an acid trip starts to turn bad, so I beat it back up to my office, at which point David Peacock appeared and said, "Nick, Nick, what are you on?" It was definitely time to leave: exit stage right and straight into a taxicab. I borrowed the driver's radio mike, calling to anybody who was listening to organize to defeat the system. The taxi drivers had been on a long strike and in my manic state they represented the revolutionary working class. By this time, I was well and truly gone. It seemed I rode for days and nights. Anyone who has, for the first time, fallen prey to a manic episode, will know that at the beginning, reality becomes super heightened, radiant, and full of meaning, just as it begins to slip into paranoid fantasy.

When my comrades caught up with me, it was clear that I was out of my mind. They put me into hospital for the first time. This didn't work because they found the hospital impossibly uptight, treating my comrades with arrogance and distaste. So they broke me out of there and took me to the country, trying, with the utmost difficulty, to keep me there and keep me fed— because I wasn't eating and was becoming rake-thin. Eventually, in desperation, they took me back to hospital— this time the Montreal General—where I was put to sleep for thirty-six hours. I woke up not knowing who I was, where I was, or what was going on. Eventually I realized it was the psychiatric ward and there were lots of crazies. And Sandy, who I christened Nurse Nicholls, was indefatigable and kept me going.

Psychiatrist: "Mr. Hutchinson, you know the expression 'you can't tell a book by its cover'? What does it mean to you?"

Nick: "No parking."

That was enough to persuade them that I was a bona-fide paranoid schizophrenic, and I was going to be moved to Ste Anne de Belleville, which is not a happy place. It's where the really crazy people are sent, very possibly for the rest of their lives. At which point, Sandy phoned Peggy, and Peggy flew out to rescue her crazy son.

Peggy arrives in a fairly frantic state, and I'm assuming that we're leaving the hospital because I'm going to be in the care of my mother, and I've been given my clothes for the first time in many weeks. Off we go—Sandy, Peggy, and I—for a jaunt around the places of Montreal that mean the most to Sandy and me. We end up at Véronique's for tea. And that's all very nice. But when we make ready to leave, where are we going? Back to the hospital?! So that puts me in a bit of a state because I'm not expecting that. We end up back at the hospital and I'm super wound-up. I say goodbye to Peggy and Sandy, and I'm back in the jaws of the orderlies. I start to stir things up. I get a couple of lads who are in there and get them wound up like me, and we're marching along down the corridor, heading for the exit. We are leaving. I'm grabbed by two orderlies and put down on a bed and thunked with two or three hefty doses of whatever it is that completely knocks me out.

I wake up in the morning from a deep and wonderful sleep (must have been the drugs they used), and on the chair by the bed are my clothes. So, I put them on, get my socks on, get my shoes on, get my everything on, and walk out of there. Nobody around. I grab the service elevator that takes me down to the kitchens, I make my way through to the front door, and I'm free. I hail a cab, and off we go to the commune in Saint-Henri. We get to the commune and I don't have any money, so I leave the cab driver yelling at me and somehow get into the flat and phone the hospital. I want to know if they are aware of my escape:

I say, "I'd like to speak to Mr. Hutchinson."

And the receptionist says, "Can I say who's calling?" I say, "Mr. Hutchinson."

"Oh, thank you, Mr. Hutchinson, I'll go see if I can find him."

(Pause)

"Oh, Mr. Hutchinson, I can't find him." "Okay, bye."

And then Peggy phones the hospital and "Mr. Hutchinson isn't here," so she's in a total panic. Anyway, she finally arrives at the commune and all the other communards come in, and it becomes an intervention with serious discussion:

"I don't want to leave Montreal. I don't want to go back to England."

"But Nick, you really should. We're sick of looking after you."

On and on and on . . . The psychiatrist from the hospital, the same one who'd been ready to commit me to a long-term mental institution on the basis of my reply to his book-by-its-cover question, diagnosed me as paranoid schizophrenic. After meeting my mum, he figured he was going to get a free trip to England out of this little lark because, given my state of mind, it was necessary for me to be accompanied by medical personnel. He contended he was the only person who really knew how to handle me. What a joke! Fortunately, Marie Claire's boyfriend Hymie was a practicing GP, and with serious persuasion, he and Peggy prevailed on the psychiatrist to forego his claim on the trip. Hymie would be in charge.

So, that very evening we took the flight. Peggy had bought two first-class tickets for me and Hymie, as was required, and she sat in the back of the plane. We were served champagne, orange juice, filet mignon—all the stuff that I would have loved to love but which tasted utterly revolting with the constant swigs of Largactil, the anti-psychotic med that Hymie administered steadily from a large bottle. The side effects of Largactil: twisted tongue, tightly knotted brow, blurred vision, trembling hands, adulterated taste, difficulty with speech—in short, a minor lobotomy.

It was a weird flight, and upon arrival I was whisked away to The Priory, a psychiatric home for the rich and famous just outside of London. At the very same time, Special Branch officers were knocking on Peggy's door at Manor Lodge, which was opened by Nan. They wanted to ask me a few questions because a couple of days before that all my buddies in England had been arrested. Just as in Montreal at the start of the October events, as a result of various radical actions (including some by the Angry Brigade) there had been a massive police sweep and five hundred radical leftists had been arrested. But Nan goes, "Och, he's not here. I dinna ken where he is." I was safely under the radar at The Priory, where the first thing that anybody said to me, in a low voice, was:

"You know, everybody's getting it tomorrow." "Getting what?"

"Oh, ECT." (Electroconvulsive therapy)

Throughout my hospitalisation in Montreal the dread of ECT never left me.

The next morning, there was a knock on my door. "Come in." And in comes the anaesthetist who gets you ready for ECT in her dark blue uniform. My back is up against the wall. I am ready to resist in every possible way. She gets to the foot of my bed and picks up the clipboard and says:

"Oh, sorry, wrong room."

You know, it's mind-fucking stuff. Was that a therapeutic intervention or simply a mistake? It's impossible to tell when the patient is heavily medicated, and their mind confused.

So, The Priory for three weeks. Peggy takes me down to recuperate in a hotel in Cornwall. The first thing I see on the TV there is that one of my friends— Ian, one of our Angry Brigaders—has just been arrested, and, as I look at the state of utter anxiety on Peggy's face, I realize the load that I have put on her. I really have to take the pressure off Peggy, and more than anything, get back to Sandy and Montreal.

And despite Peggy's protestations, that's what I do.

I'm back with Sandy, but now the inevitable depression that follows a manic spell is setting in. And when it happens for the first time, you don't know what it is. Why this total loss of energy? Why is everything you cared about meaningless? And you came back to Montreal expecting it to shimmer and sparkle as it did when you were full-on manic, but it doesn't anymore, it's just another grey city. I still had the remainder of the contract with the theatre school: two workshops with the English section. I did them with extreme difficulty. I barely remember anything about them.

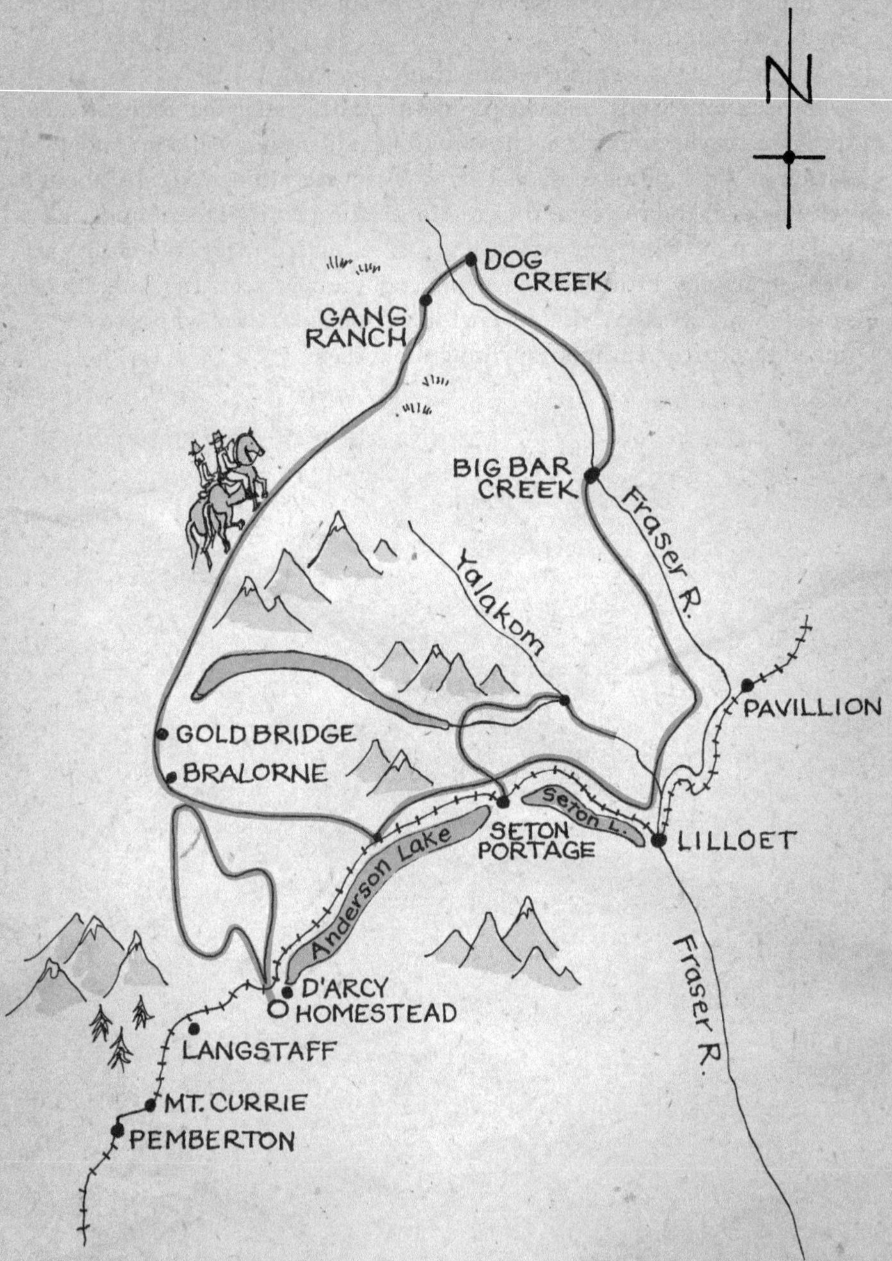
N
DOG CREEK
GANG RANCH
BIG BAR CREEK
Fraser R.
Yalakom
PAVILLION
GOLD BRIDGE
BRALORNE
Seton L.
SETON PORTAGE
LILLOET
Anderson Lake
D'ARCY
HOMESTEAD
Fraser R.
LANGSTAFF
MT. CURRIE
PEMBERTON

D'ARCY/LANGSTAFF
1971 ~ 1972

CHAPTER 6

British Columbia

And then it's thumbs out West. This is 1971. I was emerging from my depression to a more level state of mind, and realizing that my identification as a Québécois was a fantasy and that I needed to do theatre in my own language. Sandy even more so. So, my next move was to track down the San Francisco Mime Troupe, an agitprop political theatre. We hitchhiked out—Ontario laboriously, Prairies endlessly, a welcome break with Sandy's family in Winnipeg, and on and over the Rockies until, "Whoa!! British Columbia looks like a pretty cool spot." We ended up in Vancouver chez Robert Morrison, an old classmate of Sandy's, who'd been kicked out for being too much of an individualist. He persuaded us to help him finish the tower he was building at Langstaff Farm, a classic back-to-the-land hippy commune.

So, Sandy and I stuck out our thumbs one more time to get up to the farm, which was in the mountains a few hours from Vancouver.

That we'd survived together through the ordeals of this journey, the roller coaster of the October events, and then my breakdown, was a testament to Sandy's guts, her smarts, and her love—in fact all the things that made her an amazing actress. We were also finding out that the two of us didn't miss the big city. We'd been set down from our ride a fairly short distance from the farm for a two-hour wait in Mount Currie. It's the biggest Indian reserve in BC and, "Oh my God, where am I? Am I in Spain? No, I'm in a third-world country." It blew my mind because I had never seen a seriously devastated Indian reserve. At that time the streets were mud, the log houses were ancient, managing with difficulty to remain intact, few people were to be seen—it was mainly scruffy dogs, sniffing for anything that might be food.

Fifteen miles later we arrive at Langstaff Farm. George Langstaff was a wonderful old communist farmer who read nothing but Marx and Lenin and had decided, at a certain point after his wife had died, that he was going to turn his farm over to the revolutionaries of tomorrow. Thus, Fergie, Robert, Flower, Doug, Jerry, Ian, Yippee Joe, Sandy, and Nick had all gravitated there because this was one of the first back-to-the-land farms. Some were trying to get work; nobody had any money, but everyone scraped by . . . story of a commune. I kind of loved it, but I didn't really like the geography. It was in a very narrow valley with a road and power lines and a railroad track, and everything was tight.

I met a significant part of my future at Langstaff Farm. Patty White showed up with her daughter Brandy, fresh from her travels in Mexico. I was nailing some siding onto Robert's tower and I looked down to see her: "Oh, my God, I'm going to have a baby with this woman." What an extraordinary thought to have, seeing someone for the very first time. What was it that made such an impression? There was her beautiful four-year-old daughter Brandy (our host Robert's daughter), her tanned Mexican look, her long, flowing hair—but none these justified the jolt I had got from her arrival. We didn't exactly fall into each other's arms.

There was a lot of discussion of political topics and the direction of the commune, and Patty and I found ourselves agreeing for the most part. Besides, there was Sandy to whom I was devoted— although since my return from England there was a gap between us in the physical realm, and it was clear that Patty was on the point of stepping into that gap.

Fergie, the guy with the longest hair in the commune, had a horse, Dingaling. I have always had a passion for horses. My first memory, apart from riding the donkeys on Hampstead Heath, was sitting up on top of a workhorse, holding onto the hames at Mr. Bishop's farm in Dorset, and loving it. Then I rode whenever I could and always bugged people to let me ride. When I was bucked off for the first time by Strawberry, the pony, I broke my arm badly. After that, I rode a bit but never with great confidence. I had arrived now in my youthful dream of cowboy country; I imagined "packing my grip for a farewell trip" for at least two or three days and . . . Fergie had a horse called Dingaling.

"Well, we should do a trip, eh Ferg?" "Yeah."

"Well, what are we gonna do for a horse for me?"

"Oh, well, let's go borrow a horse. There's gotta be a horse somewhere. There's hundreds of horses."

We comb the valley. We both have hippy-long hair and don't exactly look like normal horse people. And if we don't have a joint hanging out of our mouths, we stink like one. Nobody would lend us a horse, until we arrived at Harry Kenyon's ranch. There, his fourteen-year-old son, Linz, was writing his first hit tune on the guitar.

Harry, a five-foot-four cowboy from Lancashire, the son of a vet, had come to Canada to seek his fortune, robbed a bank in Winnipeg, escaped to Alberta, and become a cowboy; he fixed horses up when they got sick or shoed them whenever needed. Someone had said, "Hey, Harry, you want this horse? He's just plowed what's-his-name into the fence, and he threw what's-his-name over there, and banged up what's-his-name, and I think he damn-near killed the other guy.

Nobody wants to ride him." So, Harry took him. The challenge was irresistible. Snake.

Harry broke Snake because he was an excellent horseman; he used him to perform ultimate feats like chariot-racing in the Mount Curry Rodeo, then running him into the bucking chutes, and then riding him as the "pick-up" horse, all in the same afternoon. But he still had an eye to sell him. So, when we came to borrow a horse, we said, "Harry have you got a horse? Please Harry. You've got a bunch of horses, and no one will give us a horse."

He says, "Oh, I got a horse. He'll take you up the mountain and back down, if he don't kill you." "What's his name, Harry?" "Snake."

And I'm starting to go, "Oh my fucking God." We have to round up all his horses and drive them into the round corral. Harry, standing behind

Snake

the fence, dabs a loop on Snake, who stood four square with every muscle quivering as the rope hits him, and then, very gingerly, Harry puts on the halter.

"Here. Take him home with you and come back tomorrow and we'll put some shoes on him."

It was terrifying. I walked him home and brought him back.

"Well, boys, we'll have to build a squeeze for him cause he won't pick his feet up any way else." We build a squeeze. He still won't pick up his feet.

"I'll have to get a tranq." Snake doesn't like needles, but Harry gets one in him anyway, to no avail.

So then Harry says, "Go down the road to the store and get Georgie Jones. We'll throw Snake on his side and hog-tie him and put the shoes on there."

The whole process was hard to take for a genteel Englishman, but wrestling this magnificent horse first to his knees and then to his side— eyes flaring, breath laborious—was hard to stomach. But we do it, throw the horse, put another tranq in him, which finally settles him down, and tie up his feet. Harry puts his shoes on fast and furiously which is no easy matter when all four feet are tied tightly together and the horse has muscle spasms when you least expect it. Almost as soon as Harry's finished, Snake sort of stumbles up.

"Okay, kid, throw your saddle on, take him out on the back road, and get on him quick. Just stay on." We took him out on the road. I tried to get on him. No way. No way. He wasn't letting me get anywhere near him.

"Harry, couldn't I just take another horse? I mean, what's the big deal?"

"Aw, he'll be alright. Just bring him back tomorrow. We'll put the "running double W's on him, throw him on his nose a couple of times, and he'll be fine." Dictionary definition of Running W's:"a dangerous stunt to trip a horse."

Next day, we did that.

You put hobbles on the front legs, run a rope from hobble to hobble through the cinch, and then back to the driver. You drive the horse until he bucks, and then you pull his front legs out from under him and drop him on his nose. This was Western horsemanship; we were getting a full-on lesson. It was wild and scary, but Harry was a master and the ordeals of the day before had toughened me up. And there was something in the "running double W" process that connected me to Snake, which in the long run I think was important. We dropped old Snake three or four more times and then Harry said, "Okay, that'll do. Put your saddle on and come in the kitchen, Nick." And he poured six glasses of rotgut red wine. He took one and said, "Drink the rest. Get on him quick and be light on his mouth."

And I went out there with terror in my legs. Snake was an earthquake waiting to happen. I got on him quick . . . and all was well.

So, off we went to the hills, stopping to tighten Fergie's cinch, whereupon Dingaling got stung by a couple of wasps and took off at a gallop. I had no option but to gallop after them with only one thought in my mind—*stay on*. Which I managed to do for six hours until we reached our first camp. Lying on my bedroll, looking up at the stars, I dreaded the next morning. Would he let me on? But he did. And in the end, when Harry asked me to deliver him to yet another potential buyer, I said, "Oh no, Harry, sell him to me. What do you want for him?"

"Oh, I don't know. A hundred and twenty-five and I'll throw in the saddle. Will that do ya?"

It did. So that was the end of San Francisco and the mime troupe.

My saddle built and sold to me by Harry Kenyon in 1971.
Photo by Linz Kenyon

Sandy, Nick and Fergie Homesteading

CHAPTER 7

Homesteading

There was a cabin in the woods a couple of miles shy of Anderson Lake, near the Darcy Indian reserve and importantly the Darcy General Store. The owners, the Brotherstons, offered Fergie and me the place to caretake. We were well and truly in the bush—trees all around, just a few odd spots cleared for a barn and a couple of corrals, a chicken run, and a rudimentary two-room cabin. They gave us a Jersey cow called Bunderella. We had chickens, three pigs—Ham, Bacon, and Pork Chops—and two horses. We had Fergie, Sandy, and Nick in this tiny little cabin, sometimes joined by Patty to make up a foursome (more friends than lovers, though I was still seriously smitten). Sandy and Patty got on famously. Patty came and went and then disappeared, as she was wont, to Mexico. I never knew why. And then Peggy arrived. Stalwart Peggy. Intrepid Peggy. Coming to the most outlandish Nick scene. And she was full-on, churning the butter, doing the whole nine homestead yards.

But then a few months into our homestead reality, really shocking news came from Montreal and a couple of our commune comrades.

Marie Claire and Hymie had overdosed and died. That was an enormous blow to Sandy and me. Marie Claire, who had introduced me to Bob Dylan back in Strasbourg and with Véronique had established the Theatre Commune and been one of our strongest voices, and Hymie—gentle, wise Dr. Hymie who had kept me together on the flight back to England. How could this have happened? In the period since leaving Montreal and the months in our homestead, the fires of the revolution had died. Everyone had to find their own way forward, some had joined the Maoists, some the evangelical church, we had joined the back-to the land movement, but some like Marie Claire and Hymie had opted for Heroin, whether their death was accidental or intentional we shall never know.

Otherwise, it was a very pastoral existence. It was the first time in my life that I suffered no boredom. There was always something to do. And always something I liked to do; whether it was looking after the animals, chopping wood, fixing the fence, it was a full life. And an absolute epiphany to be out of the city.

Sandy and I were sort of splitting up. We were a threesome with Fergie and Sandy and Nick. And sometimes a foursome with Patty and Sandy and Fergie and Nick. But we were always good friends. Sandy finally took off to the city, which is where she met up with Ian from the commune, with whom she became pregnant. Fergie and I had an amazing week when his daughter Winona, a babe in arms, was dropped off by her mother, Michelle, on these two long-haired hippy dudes. We had to learn how to look after the baby, how to change her diaper, how to do the bottle—all those basic things of life.

And at the same time, it was snowing. Bunderella, the cow, was about to calve, and then she disappeared. We knew it was close to her time but because of Fergie's baby we had to take turns looking for her. We looked and we looked, and it was deep, deep snow—four feet of snow. I finally found a few tracks that had escaped the relentless snowfall and eventually found her licking her dead calf in the middle of the woods. It really was one of the saddest sights, and has stayed with me. We had the baby at the cabin, so everything had to be done by just one of us. Getting Bunderella away from her dead calf was no easy matter with snow up to her belly but painstakingly we got her out of there.

We had to milk a heck of a lot of milk, and it was the first time we'd ever milked! So we started selling gallon jars of milk to the women on the reserve in D'Arcy. We'd ride there with two, two-gallon jars in each of our saddle bags and have long, fascinating conversations with the women, who might be in the process of hanging their catch of fish to dry, suspended from the ceiling, or puttering around the kitchen section of their dark cabins getting the evening meal together. Sometimes we'd drop off a gallon with old Shorty, a classic old native hunter-philosopher, who could hold us rapt with his many stories and yarns.

And then, it was time to do the pigs, Ham, Bacon, and Pork Chops. Pigs are very endearing animals. It's true they are greedy at feeding time, but they are very smart and we had become quite fond of them. We dreaded what we had to do. To make matters worse, they took it upon themselves to escape from their corral the night before the dreaded day, and spent that night in the woodshed. The next thing we knew, they had joined us for breakfast in our little cabin.

Okay, so you need a bathtub, which you fill with water, with a fire underneath. And you have to heat the water to just under boiling point to scald and scrape them once they're dead, which was very difficult because it was snowing. Once the temperature was reached, it was time for the first execution—and then one by one we had to stun 'em, shoot 'em, grab 'em, haul 'em up, submerge them in the bath, and scrape them. But for the fact that at every second there was another essential action to be undertaken, I don't know if I could have kept going. Fergie was tougher and kept the process together. I was constantly reminded of the young couple in one of Hardy's novels who went through a botched pig kill, where the deafening screams of the pig would not stop. Whenever I had a squeamish moment, Fergie, with his ever-optimistic, delightful toughness, would pull us through. We had very good pork. Very good bacon, very good chops. Delicious. So, we did well. We had food; we had milk, we had eggs, we had meat, and we baked bread.

In the spring, we had to leave our little place to its owners, the Brotherstons. We found the remains of a beautiful log house up a logging road which belonged to a logging company. So, we squatted that house. But our longer-term plan was a big pack trip with the horses, like all cowboys should, to the Cariboo. The Cariboo is wild country, northwest of the major populations of BC. it was the scene of the Great Gold Rush that followed the California Rush. Thousands arrived with dreams of golden wealth and there was, for a short time, "gold in them thar hills," and even now prospectors pan some of the rivers. But after the Gold Rush was over, the Cariboo became a ranching paradise, with big and small operations dotted along the great waterway of the Fraser River with cattle being driven to the pasturelands on the plateaux of the Chilcotin (the high country to the west of the Cariboo).

To finance the trip, we competed in the Mount Curry Rodeo, which is a spring event. The Mount Curry Rodeo is nothing like a conventional rodeo, which has a strict programme from bucking horses and bull riding to various roping events and the inevitable rodeo clowns. At Mount Currie, one of the main events was horse racing. We had ridden Snake and Dingaling, a half-day ride on a full-out trot to Mount Currie, and our aim was to ride in every race. And, because our horses were in super shape, we won every race. Whether it was Dingaling or Snake in the lead, the other would be just behind. We made some money and that's how we financed the Cariboo trip.

So, down to Vancouver to buy supplies, and into the Army and Navy Store. I'd had long discussions with my father, Jeremy, discussing the fine points of the law. In one of his cases (involving a famous picture being taken from the National Gallery by a pensioner who held it hostage to get the government to stop charging pensioners for their BBC licence), he had won by convincing the jury that there was no intent to steal. You had to prove intent. So, Fergie and I were in the Army and Navy Store and came on this really nice .22 rifle. You need the .22 for birds and that sort of thing. Anyway, I said: "Okay, Ferg, let's go." We picked up the .22 and walked out of the store holding it in front of us, and nobody stopped us—if they had, we would have had to convince them we fully intended to return it.

And then we prepared. Our trip was crashed by a fellow by the name of Steve—our age, blond—who came on the scene from nowhere. He thought what we were planning to do was amazing, and he wanted to do it too. So, he went and bought a horse and we somewhat grudgingly said okay. We weren't going to stop anybody. It's a free world. But this added a further complication. And the proof of the pudding was somewhere up in the hills where I came across an old cowboy. Checking out where we were going and what we were doing, he said:

"How many of there's are you?" "Well, there's three."

He spat and shook his head. "That's no good," he said.

It's true, you know, because it always ends up two against one. It just does. And it did. You know, in the simplest littlest things—whether it's who's doing the dishes, or where you are going or whatever you do. It just doesn't work.

We start to pack our packsaddles; Something we've never done before. We have one big packsaddle, which we plan to rotate among our four horses (by then I have acquired another horse, Jigs). We fill the pack up with all our stuff, and throw it on Snake, at which point he staggers. And we go, "Whoa, whoa. Take it off. Repack. We don't need this. We can't take this. We've got to have this." Total repack.

A few days later we are into country approaching the Cariboo.

And we get really nasty weather. Soaking wet and cold, and not sure where we are. Our rations are low, Steve has glandular fever, we're trying to eat chipmunk because we haven't got anything better, and it's disgusting. It's tough. But the weather's changing now, and it looks more promising. Steve figures he can make it. We pack our stuff and plan the next part of our journey, which is all guesswork, and decide, "Well, let's have some dope pancakes in the morning. We need a reward." We have plenty of leafy dope even if our cigarettes are running low.

First thing in the morning, I'm meant to go ahead and find the trail. I cook myself a good handful of dope in a pancake and I set off on Snake. I get to a crossroads, and right down the valley at the very end is the most majestic buck. I mean, just the most beautiful thing in the world. "Okay, Snake, let's go!" And we gallop down the valley and of course the buck turns and runs off, and we go and we go and we go.

Obviously, I'm getting a little stoned, and when he's disappeared out of sight, I rein in Snake. "Okay, where am I? Where am I?!" And then, "Oh God, those guys are going to be coming." I'm starting to get the stoned jitters. I'm lost. I'm in this thicket of woods and they're starting to gradually close in. They close in. Finally, I am so closed in, I tie Snake to a tree and work my way down the hill looking for a road, which miraculously I find. With a stick, I write STOP! in the sand on the road. And I turn around and go, "Oh . . . where . . . . is . . . Snake?" So, then I've lost Snake and I can't find him. Oh, insanity. Total insanity. And then, at last, amidst the tight thicket of trees, I see his head nodding, half asleep against a tree.

Back on Snake, I ride down to the road. Somehow I connect with my pals and for the rest of the day we ride into a long valley. We later discover it is most appropriately called Lost Valley, because we were definitely lost. It's starting to get a little bit evening-ish, and we stop a minute, and I look and there is a deer standing in range to me, and I shoot it and we've got food. It was a lucky shot because I'd only really had a few attempts with a 4.10 shotgun at the odd bird when I went hunting with my dad as a ten-year-old, but there was somehow a magic connection between the buck that I'd chased that morning and the deer that appeared at the end of the day.

We sit for three days or so, "smoking" the deer on a tripod. And eating. And getting stoned. And then we pack the meat that's left, get onto our saddles and head on. A day and a half later, we reach a beautiful line cabin—the last spot on the high country before we start our descent to The Gang Ranch and the Fraser River. The Gang Ranch is the second biggest ranch in BC, and has various reputations. Some not so good as others. But by the time we have done however many weeks on the road, it has acquired all sorts of the most magical, mystical, wonderful things. Our mail is going to be there. There is going to be a store. We are going to get cigarettes and beer. And every other fantasy in life. The Gang Ranch, here we come! We've survived and we're coming down.

We were coming down and it was becoming a difficult and treacherous descent off the high plateau. Steep downhills are difficult for horses. There's stress on their backs. They don't like it. We were high as kites. Our packsaddle rigging, together with the long, steep downhill, was beginning to sore our packhorses of that day, Snake and Dingaling. We should have been more aware. And then up the road comes a pick-up truck with three real cowboys looking at us, at our hair styles, and the meat on our saddles. Glad to see some human faces after all this time, we say cheerfully, "Hey, where's the ranch?"

Eyeing the meat hanging off our saddles, measuring the length of the hair on the heads of these durn hippies, the cowboy laconically, with an undertow of menace, replies, "Just keep on headin down." And off they drive.

It was about as typically unfriendly as it could be. We were hippies, or so it was said. I never once considered myself a hippy—okay, maybe I had long hair and smoked marijuana. But to equate us with the flower children of San Francisco, following the Grateful Dead from concert to concert and all the media inventions about them was absurd. At this time, hippies were grudgingly accepted in the cities— much less so in rural BC.

Of course, there was no mail, no store, no beer, no cigarettes. Our fantasies had nothing to do with reality. We had imagined a magical, mystical ranch that turned out to be one of the least popular and least friendly ranches of BC. We were begrudgingly allowed to eat our lunch there on condition that we "Ride on out of here!" afterwards. The only option was to keep going down, down,

Single-lane suspension bridge crossing the Fraser River. Photo by Doug Matthews

down to the Fraser River. And then over a huge bridge into the outpost town of Dog Creek—the only place for miles where we could restock our supplies.

We arrived in Dog Creek and our horses were sore, we were exhausted, we'd got no money, we'd got no mail . . . so we had to hay. It was haying season. We threw bales for a few days, making some money, and getting our own food. We stayed in a farmer's shed.

We had two horses that were sore and couldn't make the trip, so one of us had to drop out. For some reason it was Fergie. I was stuck with Steve. I had one of the rideable horses and so did Steve. It was Ding and Snake who were sored, and I had my other horse, Jigs. We should have had an extra horse to ease the pack load. We live and learn.

Fergie stayed with the horses, and Steve and I started on the return journey. For the first leg we kept to the east bank of the Fraser until we reached the funky Big Bar Ferry, where we coaxed our horses onto the platform that was the ferry. We crossed the Fraser again to the west bank, a bank that sits high above its river (like an endless cliff), and we began following amazing trails heading towards Lillooet. The terrain was way more open than the country we'd been in, so there was the combined exhilaration of being on the last leg of the journey and riding an easy, open path. But of course, there was tension. Steve and I had never really got along, and now it was increasingly touch and go. We both needed Fergie, who could always be counted on to keep things light. Ever since the Gang Ranch things had not run smoothly and neither of us had any idea what to do when the trip was done. In a happier moment, the thought of what we had done and what we had learned and where we had been, was cause for celebration. All I remember of the end of the trip was plodding along a broad, dusty gravel road not far from Lillooet.

Net City Rock Opera. Melanie Ray, Jane McDonald, Suzie Astley and Sandy Nichols

CHAPTER 8

Net City

By the end of that trip, I was starting to think it was time to do some theatre again. So, off to Vancouver, where I reconnected with Patty with whom I was still hopelessly in love, and fatefully she became pregnant, but kept me guessing as to whether the father was me or her great friend and admirer, Paul White. Different circumstances to the paternity issues I'd confronted surrounding Stéphane, but the central question was the same: how much does it matter? That question dogged me for years. As the pregnancy progressed, Patty and Paul became closer. I took off for a whirlwind visit to Peggy, during which time Patty gave birth to a beautiful son with Paul White in attendance.

Of course, I had initially come back to the city determined to do theatre. The emotional confusion with Patty was a sidebar to that determination. I had reconnected with Sandy, who now lived in Vancouver, and who was also pregnant and as keen as I was about getting back to theatre. One day we were driving through Vancouver with our old friend Robert, whose tower we had sided:

"What should we do?" one of us said. "How about *Mahagonny*?"

"Good idea!"

Mahagonny is the Bertolt Brecht and Kurt Weill opera whose subject is four Alaskan loggers coming out of the bush to the "City of Nets," a Las-Vegas-like pleasure dome. It seemed very relevant. I'd known it forever—we'd had the record at home.

Sandy and I were looking to discover the Vancouver theatre scene. We didn't know anything about it, but it occurred to us that for this show we needed to bring together the alternate theatre scene and the local rock scene. I figured it had to be a rock-opera, and we would need somebody to rewrite or adapt the music and the script. So Sandy and I created our version from the record sleeves literal translation.

We recruited David Petersen, a member of the principal alternative theatre company called Tamanhous, Catherine Hahn, an artist and designer, and Jerry Silver, our lead guitarist, who went out to look for the musician to write and adapt the music. David and I worked on a grant to fund the venture. Jerry led us to Doug Dodd who was holed up in a burned-out acid-rock-band house near Richmond. If you met Doug on the street, you wouldn't imagine him a rocking

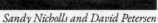

Sandy Nicholls and David Petersen   *Nick and Victor Young*

keyboard band member or someone who would live in that house. He had a combination of childlike innocence and professorial authority.

I say, "Hey, Doug, listen to this record. I want to see if you'd want to handle the music."

He listens intensely to the whole original recording of *Mahagonny* and says, "Why not?"

The Kurt Weill score is a quite complicated piece of music, and I was impressed and slightly alarmed at Doug's reaction. But there was no reason to worry; Doug took to the project with skill, creativity, and unruffled good humour.

And that was Doug's first of many gigs for the theatre.

We filled out the company and band, and Christopher Newton gave us rehearsal space at the Vancouver Playhouse. We rented the Workman's Hall, a union hall on Pender Street whose walls were covered in murals of industrial life in BC. It had a stage and a dance floor, which we set up with tables and chairs in "cabaret style," and actors and audience shared the tables. One audience member dropped bad acid into Petersen's drink one night, and his character's progress towards death was terrifying. He fortunately made it to the next day's performance, but definitely the worse for wear.

Net City, as we now called it, became a bit of a cult piece. We only did it for a few performances, but it caused a stir. Sandy played Jenny the whore, and she was eight months pregnant—sexy as hell with a great big bump. Patty was running the follow spot with our newly born son, Darcy, in a basket at her feet. By this time, we had partially reconciled, and I was currently weighing heavier on the paternity scale. It could shift at any moment and her old buddy, Paul White, could be the prospective Dad, there was nothing to be done and given my experience with Sylvianne and Jean Louis I was beginning to think that Paternity was less a question of sperm and more to do with love.

My most difficult job in the whole run was preventing the cast from getting stoned before the second act.

Patty White with Darcy

Stan Persky wrote in *The Western Organizer*:

"Although Net City (a net of whiskey, prostitution and prizefighting made to catch the gold that flows from Alaska) is roughly in the style of current pop operas, there are important differences. Unlike *Jesus Christ Superstar*, The Who's *Tommy*, and UBC's recent rock-version of *Macbeth*, *Net City* doesn't drug the audience with song and dance. It's entertaining, yes, but it also takes a penetrating look at society. Its content makes *Net City* an important advance in the use of this form of theatre. And it's definitely an alternative to Vancouver's slick downtown theatricals . . ."

The Georgia Straight said:

"If the powers that be on the O. F. Y. and L. I. P. [government granting bodies] selection panels are looking for some worthy organizations, they should take a look at *Net City* and think about channelling more of their "taxpayers' money" into the Music and the Theatre Co-ops. Organizations like this give weight to the belief that everything did not stop in 1968, not everyone has moved to the "country" to live on welfare and grants and indulge in "crafts" while their crops grow. Far more people remain in the city and at least some of them are trying to come up with some viable alternatives to the existing structures; support them whenever you come across them."

Fallow is as important to art as it is to farming. *Net City* was the thing I came back to from being a back-to-the-land, horse-owning freak. The way the play came together with the actors, musicians, and designers was a prototype for how we would eventually work at the Caravan Stage Company, and many of the *Net City* gang would become key members.

In bipolar disorder, a relapse is the reappearance of depression or a manic/hypomanic episode after a period of wellness. It's sometimes predictable but often strikes unexpectedly.

CHAPTER 9

Relapse

C o-op Radio, another just-formed co-op, offered me a job which didn't pay much, but which allowed me to get the *Net City* soundtrack recorded. Flower, who I had met upon arriving in Vancouver two years before, had gone off the twist. When we first met, we got caught on camera by *The Province* newspaper dancing wildly in the street in Gastown. It was on the front page the next day. And now Flower is in full manic gear. And Nick, who thinks he knows exactly what's going on and can therefore help, instead gets kind of pulled in. Okay what happens is, when you hit the manic phase, as I had done in Montreal, and then eventually level out, your risk of relapse is very high within the next year or two. Someone else with that manic stuff going on can trigger you into that relapse in the blink of an eye.

Despite our best efforts, Flower gets taken off to Riverview, a turn-of-the-last-century mental asylum. Try as we might, we can't get her out of there, by which point I realize I too am at risk—speedy thoughts and sleepless nights. At the same time, Robert Morrison, Brandy's dad, who had sent us off to build his tower at the Langstaff Commune, is bedridden with something like mononucleosis, and Patty is having to taking care of him. So I take our infant son Darcy, and we head off towards my old haunts in the D'Arcy Valley: the Brotherston Homestead, the house we had squatted, the D'Arcy village, and the creeks and meadows and memories lying between. My thoughts are starting to accelerate and I'm just managing to keep rational when a good friend of ours catches up with us to say that Robert has recovered, and Patty would like Darcy to come back to her. I am still sane enough to be mightily relieved to hand Darcy over before anything gets out of hand, and he goes back to join his mother and sister, Brandy, who have by this time moved to Mission, a small town outside of Vancouver.

In my first episode of manic depression in Montreal, I was totally unaware of the condition. No one had really explained it to me or given me an inkling of what attended the follow-up, which is to go down the tubes to depression. Going up to D'Arcy, I probably wasn't yet in full manic gear (nowadays, they call it hypomania) but I was very close to the edge. I figured the valley was the place to attempt coming down.

Visiting D'Arcy and Anderson Lake, all the places I had been two years before, shimmered in the light of my hypomania. But I knew I had to come down to earth, and so spent time eating roots and leaves and following my own medicinal instincts. I managed to come down from the precipice of mania but had forgotten how far down the inevitable swing would be.

The next thing on the agenda, because life is remorseless, was that I had agreed to go back to the National Theatre School in Montreal to do a student production of *Love's Labour's Lost*. I had a bit of trouble trying to figure out what the heck this play was about for nowadays. My theatrical mind, fragile as it was, was still in *Net City*. And what a contrast to *Love's Labour's Lost*.

Arne Zaslove had invited me. He had followed Joy Coghill as the director of the English section, and I had known him a little bit and liked him a lot. He was very supportive, and there was a really good group of students who were excited and ready to go. The problem was, I had this *idée fixe* that somehow masking the four men and the four women in *Love's Labour's Lost* was going to take it to another level. I'm not sure that I knew which level it was. Things got slowed down by the manufacture of the masks, and I didn't really have any process behind me to explore masks in Shakespeare. They took a lot of the designers' time and, of course, eventually we abandoned them. It was a really good lesson in not preconceiving anything.

I was going down slowly, not a happy person, forcing myself to do the work as best I could. And we just scraped through and actually, the play illuminated itself by giving its last moments to the ordinary people and the owl, after the aristocrats had played their sexy games.

> *When Isicles hang by the wall,*
> *And Dicke the Shepheard blowes his naile;*
> *And Tom beares Logges into the hall,*
> *And Milke comes frozen home in paile:*
> *When blood is nipt, and waies be fowle*
> *Then nightly sings the staring Owle*
> *Tu-whit to-who A merrie, note*
> *While greasie Joan doth keele the pot...*

Near the end of the production, Patty and the kids arrived. We had a holiday and rented a car and drove all the way to Gaspé, to Véronique's sister. Gaspé region is a beautiful part of Québec bordering the sea and the mouth of the St Lawrence River, quite a long way from Montreal. I uncoupled the milometer on the rental car, so we actually only did ten miles for the thousand-mile trip. It saved us a lot of money we didn't have. The engine was completely screwed by the time we got back to the dealership. But miraculously, I managed to return the car, escape, and we flew back to Mission.

There was the beginning of a sense of family at that point, with me, Patty, Darcy, and Brandy. There was something really solid and warm and good about that situation. Amazing what that can do to a depressed mind.

But then I had to go off to Strasbourg again to do a student production of *Midsummer Night's Dream*. This time I'd been asked by lovely Claude Petitpierre, who had been one of my teachers. I didn't really want to do it. Up until I saw Peter Brook's famous production on swings, I had a real resistance to the play. I always wondered what all these fairies were about and the ludicrous Titania-donkey lovemaking. I desperately tried to change it. I wanted something with a harder edge like *Women, Beware Women* by Middleton, but there was no French translation. And my depression was getting worse and worse. Mania happens fast and over a short period of time, whereas depression happens gradually over a long period of time.

But eventually, I had to knuckle under and do *The Dream*. And I hated it. I was getting more depressed. I was doing my best to appear normal, even positive, but that was just a front—underneath, all was indescribably black. I hated the play, I hated my work. Then came the day we left the rehearsal room and went down to the theatre. The more I watched the rehearsal, the more I knew I was in the way; I knew I could no longer contribute anything positive. So, I got on the first train that left Strasbourg station. It wasn't even going in the right direction. It was going to Germany. I had to get back on a train that was eventually headed to Paris. Oh, the shame, oh, the guilt, oh, the self-loathing. *You do not do this! The show must go on!*

In Paris, I went and confessed to two of my old classmates from Strasbourg. Confession helped. To my astonishment, everybody covered my tracks. Claude Petitpierre was so understanding and acted fast. "Nick is in bed," he said to the cast, "with gastroenteritis." The people I stayed with in Strasbourg were brilliantly button-tight when the students came round to wish me well. A few days later, on the phone with Petitpierre:

"You know, Nick, there was nothing wrong with what you did. It was easy to finish it off. You'd done all the work. I'm sending you your money."

There was immense relief and gratitude at Petitpierre's generosity and the support I'd received from friends and family, but I was still smothered by the depression and, above all, shame at my weakness for abandoning my work.

CHAPTER 10

New Job Offers

After arriving in Paris, I stayed with my sister Eliza in the little house she had bought from Michel St. Denis, in Seine-Port. She was very kind and supportive. In fact I had received so much love and support that the depression was lifting and the full-bore forgiveness from Petitpierre took the edge off the shame of leaving the show.

Patty, Darcy, and Brandy had decided they were coming over to England, and I flew over to join them. All I wanted to do was spend time with them. We had three weeks of a wonderful visit with Peggy and Nan and the garden in Hampstead, and then down to Sussex to stay with Jeremy and his new wife, June, by the sea. It was a totally restorative and magical time.

On the very last night, Patty said, "I don't think, really, we should be a couple. I want to live with Paul White." (The same Paul who had been at Darcy's birth and who was considered sometimes as Darcy's father.)

I was stunned. We had just spent the most beautiful few weeks I had ever known, so I asked her why.

"Maybe, because he's carrots and potatoes and you're not."

I reflected for a long time on what it meant to be carrots and potatoes, but it wasn't conclusive, and back we went with the kids to Mission where I had been living with Patty before going to France. It was a disaster zone. My dog had just been killed on the road the day before I got there, and the love bird that I had given to Patty had died. It was a mess.

But we sorted it out and we trucked on. I got myself a job teaching guitar in Mission in a little music store, which was a challenge for me because I'm not really a guitarist. But I learned to teach a bit until rockers came along and wanted to learn AC/DC and Kiss. The memorable event for me was the first time I put my back out. I was carrying wood in my arms to break up for the fire, and I slipped in the mud and did my back in. I could barely move, crawling around and painfully levering myself up to hobble. I phoned up the fellow who ran the music store and said, "Look, I can't teach tomorrow. I've completely screwed my back."

"Oh, no, you've got to come in. You have to come in."

So, I went in, and I taught for the whole day on my knees. At the end of the day, I managed to straighten up enough to get myself to the local pub where one of our friends, who was quite a hard drinker, was hard at it.

It was Hallowe'en. We had a "few" upstairs and then went down to the lounge and had a few more. Then we had a few more. Then we lurched out onto the empty Mission Street. It was completely empty, and we were absolutely pissed, weaving our way down the street.

Passing the Chinese restaurant, we looked at each other and went, "We better have something to eat."

We went into the restaurant, sat down, and ordered our food.

Whereupon six burly cops came into the restaurant and sat down right at the next table with their radios going *clink-clonk, boom-foom*. And our hackles rose. And finally, I turned to them, and I said very politely, "Would you mind, please, turning your radios down? It's really interfering with our food."

And there was a sort of moment. And then my friend went up to the waitress and started to say, "Well, we're not gonna pay, if we have to suffer through this." And then, all of a sudden, we were both grabbed and hauled out of the restaurant, slung into the paddy-wagon and thrown in the drunk tank. We slept on two metal bunks in the cell. And when I woke up in the morning, my back was perfectly good. And so, yet again, "Our life is of a mingled yarn, good and ill together." So that was Mission.

By then we had moved to another house with a girlfriend of Patty's, and the house had become a feminist stronghold. Patty kicked me out. Somehow or other Sudsy (a good friend from Québec who'd been involved in *Net City*) and I moved into this little green shack at the foot of a mountain outside of Mission. In an attempt to quit smoking, we got into a strict regime of good breakfasts and then walking up and down the hill, a little more each day. Invariably, we would have a cigarette by lunchtime.

Sudsy and I would drive every week in my little Morris Minor Woody Wagon at a top speed of thirty miles an hour, to practice Tai Chi in East Vancouver. The test of a good teacher in any discipline is to understand how much information or how many moves a student is able to absorb, and that was exactly the brilliance of this Tai Chi master, who had been a general in the Chaing Kai-shek Army. He taught me a physical discipline that made complete sense which I was able to draw on ever after.

At the same time, Doug Dodd, who'd written the music for *Net City*, was organizing the "Brass Tacks Choir" involving a number of *Net City* players, and Sudsy and I became the bass section, along with David Petersen.

That summer, I arranged for the Brass Tack Choir to do a workshop at Langstaff Farm, the old hippy commune. Fergie and I saddled up our horses and rode from Mission up along Harrison Lake to get, eventually, within striking distance of Langstaff Farm. A few days into the journey, we'd run out of food. Fergie had spent the afternoon trying to shoot a robin with his .22, while I tried to catch a fish without any luck at all. So, we tried slugs cooked in butter and garlic and pretended they were snails. They weren't. They were absolutely disgusting. Don't ever try one.

Three days later, we made it to the farm. With fifteen or so Brass Tack Choir singers, the now almost-empty commune of old flickered briefly to life again. Darcy came to stay with me. The problem with Langstaff Farm was that you could catch dysentery from the water. We would call it "fartmouth." You got uncontrollable runs, and you had the most terrible farts. And of course, Darcy contracted it. It was diabolical. He was three. I would wake up in the night with a completely messed up bed. And, oh, this poor sick boy who couldn't eat anything, and it went on and on and on and we got really worried. Eventually, I drove him to Pemberton, bought him a hamburger which he ate completely, and that was it. He was better. So, it was always the permanent cure for Darcy:"Whatever ails you? Hamburger."

Not long after the Brass Tacks Choir adventure, I went to a party in Vancouver and had a great time with a beautiful weaver, Charlotte.

Following a strictly one-night stand, my son Carl was conceived. I was still heavily involved with Brandy and Darcy and on much better terms with their mother but couldn't envisage another child beyond them.

"No worries," said Charlotte, "I've got a guy." Nine months later she showed me a beautiful video of Carl's homebirth, and apart from a short visit with baby Carl on the steps of her Kitsilano home, our paths did not cross again for many years.

Since teaching guitar in Mission, I'd been living off unemployment insurance, and one day I said, "I'm going to get work because this is ridiculous. I will take any job that comes my way." Peggy came over for a visit and we met up with Powys Thomas, a fine Welsh actor, student of Michel St Denis, who became the first director of the National Theatre School English section. He asked me if I was interested in helping him with the acting school that he was forming at the Playhouse Theatre in Vancouver. So, I said, "Yes. Sure." Shortly afterwards I got a beautiful fifteen-page letter from Paul Kirby, asking me to be the artistic director of the horse-drawn Little People's Caravan. *"Wow?! Well, I've said I was*

Powys Thomas

going to take every job in the book, but here's one which actually solves the problem of what to do with Snake." So, I say yes to both.

I had heard about the Caravan a few years before, when we lived next door to "The Cultch" (a recently converted church, fast becoming a cultural hub as The Vancouver East Cultural Centre). I'd seen a flyer for the Caravan and thought, *"Oh, Little People's Caravan? Well . . . they're travelling through communities, which is what I want to do, but God, doing it with horses and wagons? That's awfully slow."* Because I'd had this idea of a flat-deck truck theatre.

The letter was very persuasive. I said I would check it out and went to dinner with Peter Hall (not to be confused with the Peter Hall of the Royal Shakespeare Company), his partner Michele Carrière, and Pearl Hunt, all of whom had already traveled with the Caravan. We had a great time together. We were on the same wavelength. And they gave me a more realistic picture of life on the Caravan, the nonstop hard work, the risks of the road, the miserable wages. Despite all that, they were still enthusiastic Caravaners, and I was going in with eyes open. Most importantly, this was a job for Snake.

Late in the winter of 1976, I drove up with Peter to Tappen, in the interior of BC, where there was a little place with about eight gaunt, dirty old Clydesdale horses looking at me over the fence in the overcrowded corral. Not exactly the pastoral equine bliss I had been imagining. But reality is rarely what you were imagining. I went into the house which was still a work-in-progress—plywood floors, insulation peeking out from uncovered wall studs. But it was welcoming, very collegial, and I met up with Paul and Nans Kirby for the first time: Nans—dark, beautiful, of Dutch heritage, an art student who had found in her husband Paul someone as committed and capable of creating a life of adventure for their family as she was; Paul, a self-taught horseman, wagon builder, and strategist who could talk almost anyone into almost anything. There is a wonderful moment in Dorothy Walker's beautiful film *Horse Drawn Magic* (National Film Board, 1978) where Paul is leaning close to the campfire, chin in hand and his eyes full of rumination, what could he be thinking of?-today? tomorrow,? or next year's tour?

Back in 1970, when I'd returned to Montreal for the theatre commune, the first thing I'd done was to go to the anarchist newspaper *Logos*. The newspaper had just come out with a facsimile of the *Gazette* newspaper, with the fake news "Mayor Drapeau shot by Drug-Crazed Hippy." It was a deliberate provocation by Paul (then the editor) and Nans, aimed at the very unpopular mayor of Montreal. They'd had to leave town in a hurry following this, so I never got the opportunity to meet them.

They'd crossed Canada in their funky old car and seen a lot of horses (as had I on my travels through Alberta) and while sitting dealing with their suddenly broken-down car, had come up with the idea of a horse-drawn show.

From Tappen, Peter and I set off to "log" the next year's tour. "Logging" the tour means driving the proposed route with the passenger logging in a notebook the distances between the towns, the water stops, potential places to stay, and all the hazardous or difficult hills.

I came back to the city and started to work at the Playhouse School. Powys Thomas had left the National Theatre School in Montreal because he found it too bureaucratic. He was interested in getting people with life experience and maturity. They had a different age range than a normal theatre school. My first task was directing Chekhov's *The Wood Demon* and I persuaded Powys to play the patriarch. And it was great because Powys became the teacher by example. So I didn't have to be the teacher, I could be the director. And, apart from the fact that Powys tried to seduce every single woman in the group, there was a great convivial social element in the whole process.

Around May, I went back up to the Caravan. But first, I had to get my horse, who had not been ridden or worked or anything for a long time. I pulled him out of the bush and away from his buddies and saddled him up. I had a bedroll and some saddlebags. It was going to take me one day's riding, sleep the night, and another half day, and it was over a very high mountain pass, Mission Pass. What was I going to feed Snake? It was very early spring but up on top was late winter, not much grass. I filled up my saddlebags with pig feed, because I couldn't find any oats on the way. Pig feed is very rich. Not really what you should be feeding a horse, but it's better than nothing.

We ride out along Anderson Lake to Seton Portage. And then up. And then up and up and up and up and by dusk, over the pass. *Where am I going to sleep?* I want to make as many miles as I can . . . but this is a thing you always go through whenever you're on horseback. Do you stop early? Or do you push to the end?

We are now on the top of the pass. It isn't very hospitable. Rocks and stunted trees. We are now above the treeline, and as we start to descend, darkness is falling. It gets darker and darker. I can't see anything. I know I'm on the road, a long gravel road down towards Lillooet, thinking, *I have to stop. The next place where there's a pull off, I'll pull off the road.* I pull off the road and unsaddle Snake and, *Ooh! It's freezing cold!* I gather some twigs to make a fire and Snake eats all the twigs cause he's so hungry. And I can't get the fire going. I wrap up in my horse blanket, freezing cold. When I wake up in the morning, I look up and I'm underneath a friggin' glacier waterfall that's frozen. I've been in this absolute icebox all night.

Snake and I were ready to go. *Let's get out of here!* And it was amazing. We flew. Snake had a foot-flying extended trot when he got going, like a real pacing horse. Our rendezvous was in the Yalakom Valley at a little homestead belonging to Doug and Jerry, original members of the commune at Langstaff. Paul and Nans arrived with a white truck called The Pig. We loaded Snake and drove to Tappen.

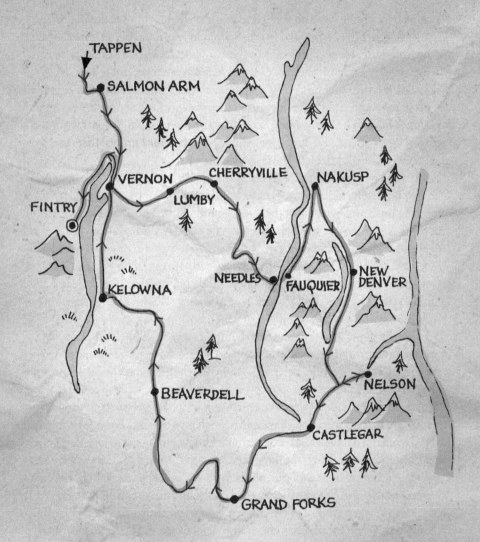

STAG KING 1976

CHAPTER 11

The Caravan

The Caravan Daily Schedule:

- Physical warm-up

- Reading and rehearsing *The Stag King*, a commedia romance by Gozzi, a
  brilliant mix of stock commedia characters in a fairy-tale world with hero,
  heroine, villain, and a magical stag. (We played in the round to a centre stage
  and then moved the action out to the perimeter against the backdrop of banners
  that connected the wagons. It kept the audience on their toes, sometimes with
  longshots sometimes with close-ups.)

- Exploration of our intended second play of the season, the story of Bill Miner

- Horse-work (each member of the company was assigned a horse to care for
  and trained as a teamster, shotgun, or outrider)

- Music rehearsals and jams

- Discussions (on many subjects, with decisions being made collectively,
  including an important debate on my suggestion of changing the company's
  name to the Caravan Stage Company— Nick and Paul's first disagreement.)

Money was tight and we ate a lot of lentils. On the plus side, I managed to
convince Sandy Nicholls and her new and lifelong partner, Jim Meers, to join
the crew on the strength of their interest in the Bill Miner story.

Packing up our four wagons for the road — the Vardo (the Kirby's family
wagon), the Sally, the Medicine, and the Hitch. Into and onto these have to go
the poles and canvases that make up our performance circle, the lights (old car
headlights converted into parcans powered by a bank of batteries). The props,
the company's bedding, tents, and personal bags, the cooking equipment
and food, horseshoes and farrier equipment, and the two goats, who will be
supplying us with milk. On tour, the same packing has to happen every time
we strike camp, but leaving for the road for the first time, it takes a lot longer.

Eventually we set off on *The Stag King* tour.

Within five minutes we had to stop; something needed adjustment. A piece
of harness. Or the news that the Canada Revenue Agency had just garnisheed

the little left in the Caravan Bank account. I began to realize, as we once more attempted to get going, that the first lesson on the road is patience.

As with our departure, our first shows were faltering and slow. We were performing sometimes once or twice in towns that were three or four days apart, so it was hard to iron out the wrinkles and strike a good rhythm. On top of that, what turned out to be a summer of rain began to threaten us.

We arrived in Lumby in the pouring rain, where we'd aimed to take a week's break to tackle the Bill Miner project. But we had to make some money. It was too wet to do outside shows, so I got us a gig at a pub, and we formed the Caravan band "Ladies and Escorts" (the traditional lawful entrance sign for women into pubs). We made some money and got our musical act together based on the regular jams between all our musical performers. Bob was the cook, and our major staple changed from lentils to beef heart. You had to learn to love beef heart—it was the cheap fix.

We did have an occasional day off. On one such day I took Snake, who was in tip-top shape, for a ride. I chose to leave the road for the ditch and softer ground for his feet, because he wanted to trot out.

BOOM, he hit a shard of a Coke bottle, and it cut across his coronary band, the main artery above his hoof. It was open and pouring blood, and I was trying to wrap it with any piece of material on hand. And this wonderful old vet, Vic Demetric, appeared (God knows how) and we staunched it and wrapped it properly. Snake was impaired and off the road for quite some time. That was a huge blow. I can't even remember who I rode after that.

Our next move was to Cherryville at the foot of the Monashee Mountains. We still had a gig at the Lumby Hotel where we'd been playing, because by then we were almost the house band. We all piled into a pick-up truck and drove back to Lumby. We were a bit late, of course, as we walked into the bar. It was utterly and totally destroyed. Wrecked. The Hells Angels, who we'd encountered somewhere between Vernon and Lumby, had come into the pub, which was owned by an ex-narc, and trashed it. Lucky for us we were late, or we probably would've been trashed too as a bunch of hippies.

That was the beginning of a pattern between us and the bikers because we were all heading in the same direction, towards Nelson where there was going to be a huge biker gathering. We arrived in Nelson, two hundred miles on, at exactly the same time—ironic, since we traveled at two miles an hour and the bikers at sixty. What could they have been up to?!

Leaving Cherryville we started our long trek over the Monashee Mountains, a long haul up with endless stops to rest the horses. But it was also the moment where finally we'd been on the road long enough to know the ropes; the stops and the starts were more efficient and there was no show. We were just travelling. Bliss.

Paul and Nans Kirby in their Vardo

Somewhere near the summit the weather was good, and so most of us were sleeping outside on bedrolls. I woke up to see our big mare, Joy, approach our soundly sleeping farrier, Doug Saba, stood over him for a while and then, very delicately but deliberately, laid a big front foot on his head. No harm done, and Doug woke up. How I wished I'd had a video camera.

So down through the Slocan. Suzie Simard was our PR-advance. But our advance publicity meant nothing as we headed into territory that had no experience of the Caravan. And you see, at this time, we really were a raggle-taggle bunch of gypsies in the eyes of the public. Some people liked the looks of these long-hairs and others muttered, "They share their women and smoke dope and who knows what else?" And the Nelson Council had refused to provide a public space for the Caravan to perform, unlike all the other places we had been. Suzie managed to get the editor of the *Nelson Daily News* to visit us on the road, and he became a firm supporter. Pushing the controversy with

On the road with the wagons

articles and editorials, the council relented, and two weeks or so before we were due to arrive, the Caravan was on the map.

After New Denver, we spent a night at a campsite where we had to park our wagons by the side of the road and picket the horses way below in a field. To picket a horse, you drive a stake into the ground and have a rope or a chain attached to the horse's leg. This was how we contained them with no fencing. In the middle of the night, we were awakened by the sound of horses' hooves pounding the pavement.

Twelve horses or more were thundering up the hill, through the wagons and onto the road heading back the way we'd come. They'd been spooked by a bear or something and pulled their chains, so stakes were flying, and the odd shoe ripped off a foot. Half-dressed and bootless, we finally caught them on the road and brought them back at three in the morning.

We arrived in Nelson, a real mix between a strongly conservative element and a vibrant artistic one, with the hippies and pot growers surrounding it. Fortunately, the site was away from the town centre, because at the same time, the entire west chapter of the Hells Angels invaded. They closed down all the merchants in the high street, erected their rock music speakers and started their biker party. They literally terrorized the town. It was not very good for our business, and we were in a state. "Oh my God, what if they come riding around where we are?!" Fortunately, they didn't. We weren't very well attended, but we got a good review from our friend at the *Nelson Daily News*.

We went to a bar one night, drinking and carousing, and a beautiful woman with a heart-stopping voice got up and sang, and my knees wobbled. It was Jude Lee. She sang in a way only Jude can sing; it reaches straight into your guts. We met, we danced, and thus began my "Jude" moment. We invited her to come and sing with us, and she came out and played a gig or two. I was hoping she'd come back with us and join the Caravan, but she didn't. We were undeniably attracted to each other, and I was truly smitten. And since Patty now was together with Paul White (carrots and potatoes), I was a free agent. Not so Jude, who with her son, Jake, was in a relationship with a single dad and his children. After the tour Jude and I met up briefly in Vancouver but given her current relationship and her kid and his kids, it was still not really on. But it was.

Leaving Nelson, heading towards Grand Forks, we stopped for our three-day break. There were two major rituals that Paul and Nans had developed over the years. The first was "Jalling the Drom," a gypsy ritual before we left winter quarters for the road. It was a "Here we go!" party and feast that brought the exhausted company together before the next level of exhaustion. The second ritual, during the big three-day break on the first full moon in August, was Bill Miner Day. Bill Miner, a famous gentleman train robber, was the patron saint of the Caravan. A grand feast of goat is prepared on the first day, eaten on the second along with much drinking, and recovered from on the third. And there's a further ritual of the "hang-up tree." Everyone hangs their representational hang-up on a tree, which was either left behind or burned. With the hang-up tree, the feast of goat, all the prep and time off our normal slog. I had a moment of realization: I had never encountered ritual outside of religious doings. I saw how important they were in unifying our community.

Leaving Grand Forks, going up another long hill, we are overtaken by a van. The driver calls out to us in a very Russian accent, "Park your wagons!" We pull over, gather in a field, and a middle-aged Doukhobor opens the back of his van. With the help of a beautiful woman, he takes out this silver tray with glasses, and a beautiful decanter of raspberry cordial which he pours out for every single person in the company.

While the tray is passed around, he proposes a toast honouring us as a travelling community with values similar to the Doukhobors. It was really moving. It was so out of the blue and so affirming. We often forget that while the mid-sixties to the mid-seventies were a time of liberation, there was still prejudice in abundance; long-haired "hippies" were not always regarded as innocent flower children, and, particularly in remoter rural communities, we were often suspected of heinous crimes. To be embraced by the Doukhobor community was a grand honour—this community who had emigrated to Canada from persecution in Tsarist Russia, thanks to the efforts of Leo Tolstoy.

By the time we arrived in Kelowna (the largest city in the interior of BC) it was September. This had been a long tour. It started to get cold, and we were worn to the bone, but we did two or three sold-out shows. The shows were finally where they should be and everything finally worked. The mayor of Kelowna became a serious supporter and found us winter quarters at an extraordinary spot on Okanagan Lake, Fintry. It was a beautiful, verdant spit of land on the west side of the lake that had once housed a major dairy farm, but was now the headquarters for the very right-wing BC Socred Party, the main powerbrokers in the province. It was another long haul to get us to Fintry. By then, fall was beginning to close in. By then, it was five and a half months on the road. Can you imagine?

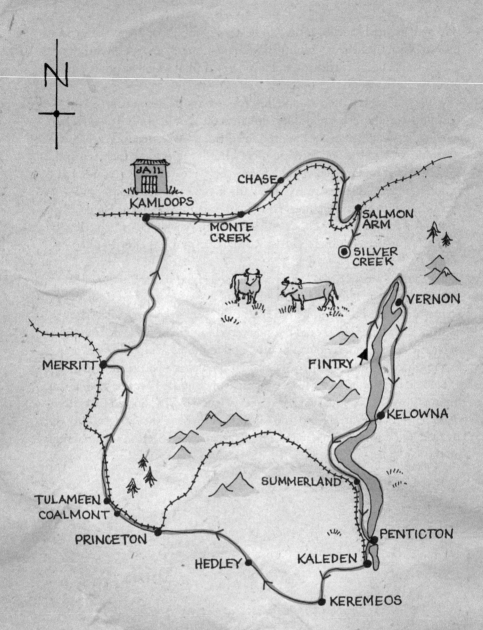

HANDS UP!
1977

CHAPTER 12

Hands Up

At the end of a tour, once everything had been put away, Paul, Nans, and family would winter with the horses, while the rest of the company would go off and try to earn some real money. I went to England and stayed with my mum and met up with our Net City/Caravan designer Catherine Hahn and her daughter, Riel. It was the last time I saw my darling grandmother Mary, who now lived with Jeremy and June and who would die in the spring.

Ron Weihs worked on a script of the Bill Miner story, based on our workshop material, that became *Hands Up!* As already mentioned, Bill Miner was an American stagecoach robber at the turn of the last century who we'd adopted as patron saint of the Caravan. He arrived in BC and lived in the Princeton area under the name George Edwards—a southern gentleman known for giving children oranges and dancing with the most attractive young ladies. Under this cover, he recruited Shorty Dunn and Louis Calhoun to rob the CPR, the completed transcontinental railroad. He was successful the first time but was caught when he tried it again. His legend was that of a modern-day Robin Hood who "never killed no-one" and who was thought to have invented the expression "Hands Up!"

Snake stayed the winter at Fintry with the other horses and was healing well. I'd gone to visit him and Paul and Nans before my quick trip England. Back from England, there was really only one thing that mattered for me: being head over heels for Jude. But at the same time, I was nose to the grindstone back at the Vancouver Playhouse School. While Powys was rehearsing and performing *King Lear* for Chris Newton with all the boys in the group, I had the girls all to myself and we tackled three all-women plays.

In early spring, Ron came back with a great script for *Hands Up!* and together with some of my favourite Caravan musicians, we cut a 45 of the top four songs from the show. During the winter break, Peter Hall had gone to the Dell'Arte commedia school in California and met Peter Anderson and brought him back. Peter was a clown, unicyclist, and playwright. He was working on a piece about Henry Ford and performed it as his audition for us, revealing himself to be the obvious choice to play Bill Miner. Sherry Bie, with whom I'd

Alan Merowitz, Peter Anderson, Peter Hall

become great friends at the Playhouse School, joined us. Sandy and Jim didn't. Sandy couldn't face a second year, though she did come back for the following.

We rehearsed the play in Fintry; the tour was going down the Okanagan Valley via Keremeos to Princeton, through the Bill Miner heartland. That was where we started getting the stories from the old people about Bill. The real stories that were constantly enriching. What a difference between the audience reactions to *The Stag King* and this. An eighteenth century romantic commedia fairy tale versus an authentic BC western outlaw story—there's no comparison.

I've found that there are shows that one wrestles with— rehearsals full of anxiety, searches for the meaning if there is one, sleepless nights figuring what to do in rehearsal next day. There are plays, on the other hand, that fit their purpose with the actor, the audience, the designers, and only need the odd touch from the director to bring them alive. *Net City* was one such and *Hands Up!* certainly another. *Hands Up!* was a joy to prepare, rehearse, and perform, and it put the Caravan squarely on the map. During rehearsals came a personal dose of tragedy. Grandmother Mary died—sure, at a ripe old age—but this was the first family loss I had experienced, so I had to discover how grief works.

The Caravan had left Princeton before I did, and as I was packing up my tent, the news came about Dorothy Walker, the wife of a doctor in Vernon. She had become enamoured with the Caravan, had done all sorts of things to help us, and had come with us for a holiday. Going up a long hill out of Princeton, where all the passengers on wagons were supposed to get off and walk, she had missed her footing getting down off the hitch wagon while it was still moving, fallen under the wheels and been killed.

There was a hard and fast rule on the road: never get off a moving wagon. We were devastated. How do we handle this? What do we do? We were between these two off-the-map places, Coalmont and Tulameen, quasi ghost-towns with just a very few inhabitants. It was hard on everyone. There was the grief for sure but there was also the shame, the sense of responsibility, and the heartbreak over the heartbreak of Dorothy's family.

Our next show was in Coalmont, and we had a day or two to breathe, to mourn, and begin to get our feet back on the ground. We had to really support Eric, who had been driving the wagon—Eric, who was one of the most experienced and careful teamsters and who was of course the most broken apart by the accident. Then there was Dorothy's family who came out, and that was very hard. They were unbelievably kind and understanding. How do you process tragedy?

And as always there's the counterpoint: *The show must go on.* We had to reschedule the date of the show in Coalmont, and we were anxious that we had lost our good PR. Would anyone come?

We set up in a beautiful meadow with a creek running through it. There was nobody around. There we were at the half-hour, dressed and ready to go. No one. At the five-minute call, still no one. And then at seven-thirty, which is when the show was meant to start, suddenly, a crowd was walking towards our circle of banners. Bob Allen from the *Vancouver Province* newspaper was there and wrote:

"Wandering around an area as rich in history as the Coalmont region and then sitting out in the open air to see those past days re-created with such flair becomes an almost supra-theatre event. You get the eerie but extraordinary feeling of having been allowed to visit some ghostly figures instead of merely watching another stage presentation. That is much the way it was for the Coalmont audience, too. For them, it was not an occasion to be "cultured," rather an opportunity to have some of their own history given back to them as pure enjoyment. Somehow, you can't help feeling that it comes very close to what theatre should be. In the pseudo-sophistication of the big city, we often lose sight of that."

And then Bernie Bomers, our new publicist, secured a masterstroke of getting the officials in the Kamloops jail to agree to a show for the prisoners on the site of the old Kamloops jail, which had housed the Bill Miner gang. The prisoners were bussed in from Clearwater complaining, "What the fuck're we doing here? Who're these long-haired hippies?" All our prop guns were checked by the prison guards, and I entered into serious negotiations to allow all the lights to be turned off during the "jailbreak" in the last ten minutes of the show.

The authorities were reluctant at first, but by two-thirds of the way in they were persuaded. The prisoners were full-on into it after the first ten minutes.

The last few towns of the tour went whizzing by at two and a half miles an hour. Lest I forget the most important part, we arrived in Salmon Arm to find Jude with her son Jake. Her suitcase in a car, she was ready for the plunge. She sang in the *"Tabootenay"*, our afternoon show—a mix of fairground, medicine, show, and music. The *"Tabootenay"* was Paul's show, and it featured him as Doctor Heart, selling Doctor Heart's Road Apple Body Balm and Skin Salve in a beautifully labeled little tin containing dried horse shit. The main seller was a potion made up from a campfire cauldron of God knows what: Doctor Heart's Perennial Wonder Cure for Whatever Ails You.

But most momentous of all, my mum Peggy arrived. Here's an extract of her description in a letter to my father and June:

"Darling J, Hi! as they say here. As a start I can say it really was the most happy and refreshing week I've had for years; it remains with me but seems almost like a dream. It gradually got light as I flew towards Kamloops, as I saw the most fantastically beautiful country of Nick's Okanagan Valley—rolling pastures, rivers, lakes, and always mountains in the background framing it all. Nick had rung me the night before, it was pouring with rain and they'd had their show rained off for the first time, but by the morning it was shiny and fine. He turned up at the airport (very small) in a red car with a new girlfriend and her little boy aged five. Surprise, surprise!! She'd driven over to spend the weekend from over a hundred and fifty miles away . . . more of that later. He seemed happier than I have ever seen him—longing for all the news and with lots to give, so you can imagine the talking was endless but somehow everything was wonderfully relaxed. I think I'll give you an account of the happenings as they came, otherwise I don't know where to begin. After breakfast at the airport, we set off for Salmon Arm and arrived by midday—a very civilized inn, the Shuswap Inn, where Nick had booked me in which was at the side of a huge playing field where the Caravan was standing. Very disappointingly for Nick, I was not to see the full "theatre" with surrounding canvas wall as, because of the weather, they decided to put the public on a small wooden baseball "grandstand" (which had a roof) and they played on the space in front (actually it never rained). We had lunch in the Shuswap Inn and I was taken down to meet the co. There seemed to be two of most names. "Hi Eric, this is my mother. Hi Peter, this is . . ." etc. I won't describe them all it would take forever and I'll keep it for when I get back.

The creators of the whole thing—Nans and Paul Kirby—are two of the nicest and most remarkable people I've ever met, they have two boys aged five and nine and are expecting another—as a family, they inhabit one caravan (the original). The atmosphere which prevails is difficult to describe—everyone belonging in some way like an enormous family. Everything was casual but extremely efficient. You can imagine I was pretty excited when the evening came; wrapped in every conceivable woolly, hat, and boots, we sat on the second step up. They time it to begin at dusk so it darkens as the show goes on. Quite amazing lighting from spots and footlights—battery filled! The four caravans in an arc are the background and the distant mountains form another.

The show was so good, I was really in tears of excitement at the end. I know one has to allow for special interest!!! But I saw it three times but I was able to be detached and critical of certain weaknesses but the overall effect was really stunning. Each performer plays at least three or four roles, they can all sing, most play instruments, and there's a lot of knock about clowning you would adore. Nick is the sheriff—with gold-rim specs, tailcoat and paunch, black hat, and a North Country accent—very funny. Also, a policeman, one or two other characters and plays his guitar on and off throughout. He's quite an actor!! There are three or four really good other actors—Bill Miner quite remarkable but the whole group really make a marvelous ensemble. The effect of the actual train robbery—Miner and his gang climbing over the roofs of two of the caravans and holding up the driver in the third— was spellbinding and wildly funny. At Salmon Arm the actual CPR ran behind the playing field and let off a hoot which drew wild cheers from the audience. It began at 7:30 over at 9:30 and by 10pm we were all in the pub by the hotel where Nick and three or four others sang for another hour and a half (earning another hundred and fifty dollars).

By Sunday the sun was in full strength—Indian summer by day, frosty at night and morning. Sunday afternoon was what they called the "Tabootenay", an open day when all are invited to bring their instruments, or pictures, or pottery, plus wagon rides for the kids and clowning and juggling!! Plus—as always—the singing. Difficult to describe in detail. In the evening—the show—and mother was invited to take part!!! So in the second act I appeared as a Canadian farmer-ess in old dungarees, check shirt

Peggy dressed to go on as farmeress

and straw cowboy hat, plus pitch fork. I had two lines in a scene where the town folk—or country folk—are commenting on Bill Miner's arrest: "the future runs straight as a barbed wire fence!" And I was there for the final chorus!! Very nervous!! Unforgettable.

The next day was the pack up, a fascinating operation, after lunch around the campfire. Snake was brushed and groomed by Nick, and we set off around 3:30 for Silver Creek. I rode with Paul Kirby on their caravan, which is the lead—Nick on Snake, one of the outriders. I must say I found their job a bit scary—Nick riding ahead with STOP/SLOW sign in his hand, stopping right in front of oncoming traffic; they have a signal system down the line to regulate the traffic behind. I moved into the little buggy around 5:30 which moves faster and so was the first in Silver Creek—by then bitterly cold! It took three hours to do the ten miles! (I warmed up in the local store.) (Silver Creek has one store and a school and that's it.) It was dark when they all got into the school playing field. First thing a hole was dug and a fire lighted. I walked one of the Clydesdales to pasture about half a mile away—about six of us in a line—back again to the camp where a stew and potatoes were being cooked. You eat standing up or sitting on a log of wood if you can find one!! You drink tea or coffee if you can find or share a mug. They wouldn't hear of my sleeping out—thank God!—and Paul Kirby had a friend in a log cabin who he phoned in the local store and I was driven, but in the standby truck which blew a tire half way there—no spare wheel—we ground two miles on a rim. So, the next three days I slept there. . .

. . . But to go back to Silver Creek and the last performance.

I'd a very restful day in the log house, sat in the sun, played snooker!!! Nick was busy setting up for the evening. I was fetched by Catherine and friends who'd gone to buy special supplies for a last night's supper.

Then I was able to see the full beauty of Cath's "theatre set up" at the end of a long sloping field. It looked magical. I sold programmes at the "box office" which was the buggy and stood at the opening gap for the customers—at least a hundred children or more absolutely agog, as the "clowns" had given them a special show in their school that day. I decided not to "perform" as I wanted to see it right through again. It got a marvelous reception and then in the dark we all had supper round the fire. The Canada Council Drama representative had come and someone from CBC and they were extremely enthusiastic, and it looks like the Council's upping the grant again and paying the cost of travelling the outfit over the Rockies to Alberta next summer.

Next day I went up to the camp to say goodbye to the troupe who were all dispersing for the winter and the Kirbys busy trying to find winter quarters."

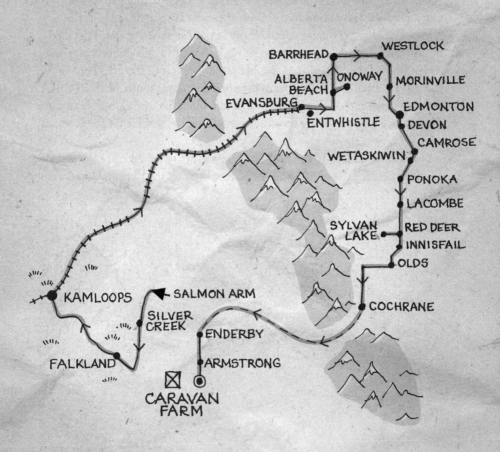

THE
COYOTES
1978

CHAPTER 13

The Coyotes

Jude, Jake and I make our break to Alberta, our cars piled to bursting with all our gear. Its most momentous for Jude, as she is leaving her family of the last two years. Alberta's the target for next year's tour. Peggy has left to begin rehearsals for Beckett's *Happy Days* at The Citadel in Edmonton with John Neville. It will be a remount of Peter Hall's production from The National Theatre in London.

Jude and I found a trailer in Sylvan Lake, halfway between Calgary and Edmonton. Peter Anderson eventually joined us and started writing what was to become *The Coyotes*. Compulsive performers that we were, we formed the "Full Moon Revue" and played bars and anywhere we could get a foot in. We were getting to know this unfamiliar country called Alberta. For instance, it gets extremely cold. I'd get into my old, beat-up Volvo and try to push the clutch in, and nothing would happen.

It took a while to learn that you had to plug in your car. The trailer wasn't exactly the warmest place on earth, so we eventually found a brand-new condo to rent which turned out to be not much better. It'd been built by Vancouver builders, who, like us, didn't have a clue.

I visited Peggy in Edmonton a couple of times and went to the first night of *Happy Days*. *Happy Days* is a total tour de force for the actress playing Winnie, buried in dirt up to her waist and eventually up to her neck. It is funny and tragic, and Peggy was spellbinding. At the interval, I eavesdropped on the bejewelled matrons of Edmonton: "Oh, very nice, but what do you think it's about?" John Neville had been artistic director at The Citadel for a few years and had seen to the construction of a beautiful new theatre, and I think the production of *Happy Days*, apart from renewing his relationship with my mum, was to challenge his subscription audiences.

Peggy proposed that the two of us should do a reading of Pablo Neruda poems accompanied by the Purcell String Quartet playing pieces of Bartok between the poems. Peggy had been intensely involved in raising money for the victims of Pinochet's CIA-supported coup in Chile. The reading was to be held in Vancouver at my old stomping ground, The Cultch. It was a daunting and nerve-wracking proposal. It was one thing to upstage my mother while she's holding a pitchfork and wearing a cowboy hat and another to sit and match her delivery and familiarity with the texts. But of course it was a challenge I couldn't refuse. John Lazarus wrote in *The Province*:

> "Everyone, including the overflow audience, appeared a touch nervous at the beginning; but Neruda's delightfully surreal humour soon warmed us and sensitized us to the serious work that followed. Though Hutchinson himself has never performed anything quite this sedate on the Vancouver stage, his readings alternated well with Dame Peggy's . . .
>
> . . . There was something astringent about the whole program: a feeling of getting to the essence of things. Some of the words were almost tragic. One heard bitter irony in Dame Peggy's delivery of the poem "I Am Staying Here," including the Chilean poet's repeated excitement at embarking on a "new history and geography." (Neruda, a member of Allende's cabinet, was killed during the junta coup.) Other strong moments included "Through A Closed Mouth the Flies Enter," a surrealistic poem of childlike questions, invoking their answers after death. The final poem, "I Ask for Silence," contained the words "I have lived so much that someday they are going to have to forget me forcibly, rubbing me off the blackboard," and ended the evening with the statement, especially memorable in Dame Peggy's splendid voice, "I ask leave to be born."

The Coyotes was progressing and preparations for the next tour were underway. I'm never happy with scripts. If it doesn't grab me and keep me, and if I can't see where the writer is going, I'm difficult. But to my great delight, Sandy came along and read the script where we'd got to so far and adored it: "This is great!" And she and Jim were coming back. I felt more confident.

We were short a fiddler. Ron Weihs had done two tours and gone back to Toronto to start a theatre. Calvin Cairns was the first to come onto our radar. Fabulous fiddler. And then, almost the day after we said,

Peggy and Nick reading Neruda

Peter Hall, David Petersen, Peter Anderson rehearsing The Coyotes

"You're in," along came Richard Owings, an equally masterful fiddler, as well as being able to play any instrument you could put in his hand. *Embarras de choix.* We wrestled with the issue and in the end opted for two fiddlers, which of course we could barely afford. But in the end it paid off in droves because two fiddles are better than one, and the Caravan Band took on a new lease on life.

For the Caravan to tour Alberta presented a whole new set of logistical problems. Between sorting and solving all the issues, transport of wagons, moving the cast, dealing with unknown towns and cities, Paul and Nans had their hands full, and they had a baby on the way. They had found a very odd house in a suburb of Salmon Arm with a cracked, empty swimming pool and a few out-buildings—"La Casa." Not the usual winter quarters we were used to.

With the growing size of the company and the steady arrival of children, the need for a permanent headquarters was becoming apparent. We needed a place to build the shows, costumes, wagons.

We needed pasture for horses. So, Paul started looking. We came up with a plan. Catherine Hahn, Paul, Nans, and I agreed to put up equal shares in a down-payment—and by this time a piece of land near Armstrong had come on the market. When my grandmother had died the year before, she'd left me her correspondence with Samuel Beckett; I sold it to the University of Texas for exactly the sum needed for my share of the down-payment. And by the time we hit the road, the deal was done. We had a farm to come back to.

On *The Coyotes* tour, we get on the road and go to Kamloops where the company is loaded onto a train. The wagons are being "trucked"—the first big move of the Caravan beyond just going down the road with horses. We're going to Alberta to be a "rider in the rain." Scene painters Don Zacharias and his current girlfriend Molly March brought this song of Randy Newman's:

> *I'm just a rider in the rain*
> *Rider in the rain*
> *Think I'll go out to Arizona to be a rider in the rain . . .*

And of course, we changed it to, "We're going out to Alberta to be a rider in the rain," little knowing how prophetic it would turn out to be. Sherry was in the company again, and Catherine brought her new partner—writer, director, and actor, Phil Savath. Catherine was on the road for the first time, playing the robotic meter-maid. David Petersen joined us, and with Peter Anderson and Peter Hall became the incomparable comedy trio playing the coyotes. The icing on the cake was the return of Sandy and Jim. Together with our newfound fiddlers, the company had reached another level.

The play is set in Alberta—a satirical take on water resources being monopolized by shadowy corporate interests, and the coyotes save the day. Paul and Nans decided that they would just do the "Tabootenay" and not the show, so they could have more time for new baby Tallis and all of the administration. Somewhere in the middle of the tour, we heard the ominous news. There had been a major fire on our newly purchased farm, and all buildings—save a little red shack, a little log gatehouse, and a granary—had burned down. This was in the days when forest fires were not a regular occurrence, so that was not considered a likely cause. But arson? No reasonable supposition. Only a few of us had actually seen the farm, so given the intensity of the tour it didn't linger long in the consciousness. Meanwhile, we were having a very wet time. It was an elemental tour. For one thing, there could hardly be two more contrasting topographies than BC and Alberta. The one is an astonishing mix of valleys, lakes, rivers, and mountains. The other after the foothills of the rockies runs prairie-like to Saskatchewan.

Full Kirby Family

Alberta is the beginning of prairie—from the Rocky Mountains to Saskatchewan. It's easier to travel the flat roads of Alberta, but we were having terrible rains and storms, and when we played Fort Edmonton, we got blown down. The weather can swoop in with force.

The culmination of the wet was in Ponoka where there is a very big mental hospital with a serious history of abuses and sterilizations. We had been at least two days out in a steady downpour when we arrived there and put up in an old ward full of baths. We all needed hot baths. What a luxury! But you couldn't help feeling like the inmates in *Marat/Sade*. From below stairs, we could hear the crying and yells of the real patients. We paid for our stay with a performance the next day of the medicine show with Doctor Heart selling his "Perennial Wonder Tonic" to the whacked-out loonies. They sold like hotcakes!

Dorothy Hénaut and her National Film Board crew followed us at the start of our tour and were there when the wagons, horses, and the company trucked back to Armstrong for the last couple of shows. *Horse Drawn Magic* is the title of Dorothy's beautiful film. It gives a real sense of all that was unique and truly magical about the Caravan Stage Company. But the "great expectation" was the new farm we'd never seen. We packed up our things, headed the five miles to the farm and down the driveway. As advance rider, I got to be the first to set foot. I trotted old Snake along a path quite far from the entrance to a beautiful clearing, at the foot of a small hill looking out over a valley which ended in a line of foothills. It felt peaceful and as far away from what would inevitably become the farm's "downtown."

Said I to myself, "This is where I want to be."

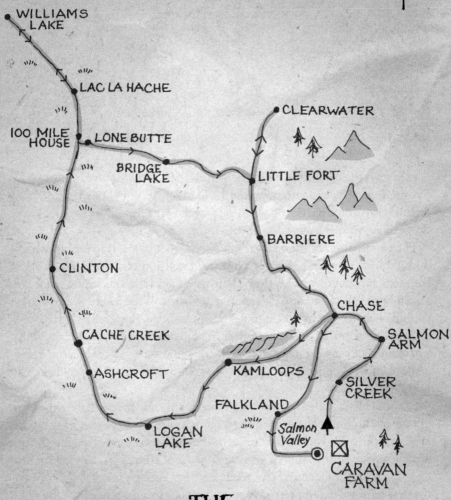

THE
GOLDEN
HORSESHOE
1979

CHAPTER 14

The Golden Horseshoe

There wasn't much left of a farm when we arrived back from Alberta. But the land was still there—and just as in the theatre, emptiness creates the possibility of something that fills it. Paul and Nans took the little red house, and for a while Jude, her son Jake, and I lived in their wagon, the Vardo. Building plans started, but real construction couldn't get underway until the spring.

Jude and I found one of the earliest log cabins in the area just up the road from the Caravan, which became our home. We teamed with Richard Owings to form a band—The Three Dollar Bill. The plan for the coming tour was to travel up the Cariboo. What is the Cariboo? Famous for the massive gold rush that followed the one in California and brought thousands of dreamers, prospectors, miners, and whores up the Fraser Canyon's corridor into a wild country. Camels were introduced to facilitate transport, but horses could not tolerate them, and the camels eventually had to be withdrawn. So obviously the subject of the show this year, which Phil Savath was going to write, had to revolve around what has become almost a mythical history: *The Golden Horseshoe*, a vaudeville musical featuring an impoverished vaudeville company that falls in with a wily old prospector who promises the pot of gold and takes them on a wild goose chase.

Richard Owings, Nick and Jude – The Three Dollar Bill

Pack up your tent, forget the rent
Leave the bills unpaid
All we need is one hot lead pickaxe and a spade
Hit the road to the mother lode no time to look back
Shuffle them worn-out shoes, shuffle away them blues
We'll be rich before we're through shuffle up the Cariboo"

From my journal at the time:

"It was from the social and ideological upheavals of the late sixties that the Caravan was spawned. The revolution so many of us expected to be just around the corner in 1968 failed to materialize. It was going to be a long haul. In those days, we thought that by direct action against the system we could bring about change. But we were new to the game, and some wound up in jail, the psychiatric ward, pregnant, isolated, drugged, and for the most part wiser.

Things don't change overnight, and if they do it's not always for the better. Revolutions can take you away from your goals more than you thought possible. It was, at the start, idealists and it always is idealists who involve themselves with the Caravan. We were searching for a means of expression that touched people, that made the experience of being together with a crowd of people fun for everyone, children, old people, performers, and public. And at the same time be stimulating, thought-provoking, worrying, and beautiful.

But why horses? Why, why horses? They were a move backward, weren't they? In time, in pace, in cost-efficiency, in man-hours, and comfort. But they were and are magic. They tell us about our past, our roots, and myths. They connect us to lost civilizations and wisdoms; they tell us of needs we are forgetting in the last part of our century; they challenge the logging trucks and tourist snakes of cars and impatient commuters to "SLOW" down and sometimes "STOP." They have maintained and sustained the members of the Caravan from the beginning of its existence. When it was winter, and the show couldn't go on, they had to be fed and watered and cared for. They brought people to see the show who had never seen theatre before because they, the horses, had stirred their imaginations or their memories of times past. They provided the actors and musicians with a life force most of them had been unaware of.

Our theatre is the field or the park, the playground, or sometimes the dump of a community. The audience sits on the ground or in their own lawn chairs. The sky is the ceiling and the background sounds are sometimes pastoral, sometimes industrial, but always there is a social reality present against which you measure your show.

When it hits the mark, you know. People are out front with their response. There's no bullshit and there is an energy that brings people close. When you fail, you think about the money."

I returned to the Playhouse School and directed *The Threepenny Opera* with the students. In the spring, I came back to our little cabin to find that Jude had split. It was a shock and I was upset, but not entirely surprised—there had been a few issues between us for a while and a two to three year span of a relationship was so far all I had managed.

But her seven-year-old son, Jake, decided to stay with me.

As spring took hold, the farm became a chaos of construction.

Paul's visionary organization of the necessary buildings was extraordinary. Two virtually volunteer builders—Derek Hawksley and Eric Procunier, both company members—and a new arrival, amazing Al, had started a cookshack, to this day the central heart of the farm. Later they built the wagon shed that would house the wagons, with upstairs a "designery" and costume shop. At the same time, Juri, illegal immigrant, was fencing the open fields. The farm had originally grown asparagus but had been neglected for a long time; in the spring, there had been enough to feed the company for a short while but now the priority was pasture and eventually hay for the horses. Jude had been destined to play the female lead, Eva, so as the company gathered for rehearsals there was a crisis finding her replacement. At the eleventh hour, Jan Kudelka—a bundle of emotional energy, a voice that belied her relatively short stature, and a memory that defied belief—arrived with her one woman show *Circus Gothic*. She blew us away with a conjuring trick of writing and performance that took us into a circus world on multiple levels, and her voice, which shook the farm. She took over the part of Eva with ease. Molly March, who had painted the previous summer, was hired as scene-painter and company member for the coming tour. She erected a beautiful teepee and despite, or

Molly March

because of, my recent break-up, her straight-forward beauty caught my eye. But our horseshoer, Zev, beat me to it.

This season, I was acting. It was a huge relief not to be directing. Phil was. Living with Jake and now my son Darcy in our little log house, we almost had a normal life. This year, to my great delight, I was to be driving the one-horse publicity buggy called "the pub bug." It was designed to go ahead of the main caravan, lay out the performance circle and deal with any issues that our advance publicist, in her car, had left behind. I saw it as an opportunity to escape the constant start-stop, endless waiting, and frustration of the wagon-train.

On my first day, in advance of everyone: trotting along after a steep downhill, we arrived at a bridge. Gathering the horse with the lines and wrapping them in my hands, we crossed the bridge without a problem. But right after, just as I was relaxing, Dale—for that was the horse's name—saw a large white rock and took off. When we came to rest, the horse was against a fence, and the wagon in a ditch.

Eventually, the Caravan caught up with me. We pulled the wagon out, set the horse back in the shafts, and I drove him another seven or eight miles until we camped. It was a sleepless night because I knew this was a runaway horse and that the next day there'd be another runaway. And so it was. Fifteen minutes after we'd been on the road in the morning, with Paul walking along at the head of the horse, we came to a bend in the road, around which came a large yellow school bus . . . and we were "gone" again. This time, we went quite a ways at full gallop, but eventually piled into some brush. We shipped the horse back home to be replaced by a lovely young Clydesdale mare, Annie, that we had bred. Her mom had a supremely gentle disposition which she had inherited, and though she had almost no training we were confident she would learn on the job.

Another lyric from *The Golden Horseshoe*:

> *We're living in the mean times*
> *Hard luck and cheap wine*
> *Sweet Jesus divine*
> *Won't you give us a break?*

That song echoed our reality heading up to the Cariboo. It was very, very hot. The horses were lathered in foam. in Lac La Hache, we were attacked by red-necked young men in pick-up trucks; we had to jump out of our bedrolls and grab metal stakes to defend ourselves. It ended in a stand-off, neither party ready to engage. We outnumbered them and they weren't expecting us to be armed.

We weren't making money at the gate. Pat, one of our actresses, to Paul: "This is a fucking prison on wheels!" Paul and Nick have a serious shouting match and musician Pat Lawson (a different Pat!) strikes up melodrama music

Molly and Nick dancing in The Medicine Show

on the newly built calliope and everybody kills the shouting match with laughter.

Between Williams Lake and Hundred Mile House, Molly and I got together. Her fling with Zev had come to an end and during that first part of the tour, as I got to know more about Molly, I realised it wasn't just a rebound attraction from Jude. One evening, when camped in Williams Lake, the furthest point on our tour, I had Brandy (Patty's eldest) staying with me. I had just put her to bed when the hot water bottle I made her started to leak. I had to act quickly, gathering the bedding, and taking Brandy in my arms close to the campfire. Molly says it was at that moment she fell in love with me.

We travelled with the pub bug and went off ahead of everyone else. We craved a short cut—not to be on some busy highway, one horse alone with roaring traffic. We took what looked like a pastoral short-cut, which turned out to be a circuitous and hilly climb; we looked down to see the wagons on the main road, way ahead. When we rejoined the company, they asked, "Where the hell were you?" It became known as the "slug bug." But the Caravan's return journey through the back country was very beautiful—we were off the main highway travelling through real "back-country."

So, we finally came back to Armstrong in one piece. It had been a good tour but hard. We didn't have the rain of Alberta, but we had the heat. The show was about the Depression, and if you do a show about the Depression, you're going to meet the depression, aren't you? Isn't that just "show karma"?

Molly and I were back on the farm together. Peggy came to the last show in Armstrong, and we had a great visit with her. We were living in a treehouse on the farm. I was full-bore to build us a house, and we started prepping.

N

SALMON ARM

CARAVAN FARM   ARMSTRONG

VERNON

KELOWNA

SUMMERLAND

PENTICTON

CALGARY

OKOTOKS

NANTON

STAVELY

CLARESHOLM

GRANUM

FORT MACLEOD

COWLEY

PINCHER CREEK

THE
CHALK
CIRCLE
1980

CHAPTER 15

The Chalk Circle

In the fall, Molly and I got a little house in Richmond near Vancouver, and Sherry got me involved with Richard Fowler, a physical theatre innovator. Six of us were working out in a church in Kitsilano under Richard, doing work based on the latest theatre practices of Eugenio Barba and Jerzy Grotowski: standing on your head, handspringing into the air, going until the breakthrough point, pushing yourself over and over again, sometimes hurting. It was a serious challenge. I had to stop being director and get my physical body involved and work my butt off. We used the extraordinary novel *Gormenghast* by Mervyn Peake as our subject and my role was Steerpike, the root of all evil. The workshop culminated in a nerve-wracking series of performances that combined *lazzis* (prepared key pieces) in the style of commedia with a completely improvised overall through line. At once a terrifying ordeal and an unforgettably rewarding experience, it had a profound effect on my vision of acting and directing.

Molly and I return to the farm to prepare *The Caucasian Chalk Circle* by Bertolt Brecht, which will be our second Alberta tour.

Southern Alberta, this time. It's the spring of 1980. Molly and I are still living in the treehouse, but we've got the beginnings of a house and we're working together as director and designer for the first time. We are also working with Catherine Hahn as a threesome, and it is mind-blowingly good. With Molly, there is a confidence and a joint creative element that will develop into our enduring relationship as director and designer.

The conversation between a director and designer is perhaps the most important. A designer who is on your wavelength can challenge you and strip you of your excesses. Molly was good at that. That was the beginning of the realization that less is more: the less there is, the more the audience imagines.

Just before going on the road, our Clydesdales got into a can of gopher poison down where Molly and I were going to build our house, at the very spot I had seen when I first rode onto the farm. Little had we known there was a can of sweet oats laced with purple strychnine, lurking in a pile of garbage. The horses came thundering up the road to where we were doing our dress-rehearsal. They were completely manic, "gone." Their noses were purple. Then they careened down the hill in front of the cookshack, in the circle, and raced around. One went down in paroxysms of convulsions and another and then another. It was terrifying.

We were at a loss. We did what we thought we had to do, which was to try and get the horses up and get halters on them and try to get them moving again. And then, fortunately, this wonderful (I called him the Falstaff of Hullcar) Len Price—this old, hard-drinking farmer/horse-charioteer, brilliant person—showed up. I don't even know how he got there. He arrived and knew exactly what we should be doing— drenching the horses with mineral oil and walking them. Shortly after, as the news spread, a few other vets appeared. Among them, Rod Gilmer and his wife Mandy, newly arrived in Armstrong, who would become major supporters of the Caravan. We walked the horses all night long. Those first three that went down— Pride, Glen, and Rye— died. That was a blow.

It took us a few days to begin to function again. The show had to go on, but we had to bury the horses, and we had to make sure the others were okay. We had to borrow a team of horses, a couple of Belgians, from one of our local teamsters. And then we had to get to the Armstrong fairgrounds for our opening. And all the kids got dysentery. We were saved by Peggy, Molly's sister, who had come to be nanny for the year. This year we had 13 kids with us for the tour. They became totally hooked on her to the point where eventually some of the parents were complaining that they weren't getting enough attention from their children!

One of the main characters in the show, the drunk judge Azdak, was played by my friend Tony Bancroft at the outset. I was to take over halfway through the tour in Fernie, way up in the mountains, where we were going to load the wagons to truck to Alberta. On my first night as Azdak, in the very first scene, Brad, who plays the soldier, approaches me as I am drinking a bottle of wine, grabs the bottle . . . and pushes it through my front teeth by mistake. My teeth rattle to the ground, and I discover, as I keep speaking, that I now have a "theriouth lithp"—not exactly an appropriate character trait for Azdak. But of course everything is adjustable, and the "lithp" was eventually eradicated.

Azdak is a great part, the best I've been lucky enough to play.

As we're heading down the mountains from BC into Alberta we wondered how the redneck audiences are going to take Brecht and *The Chalk Circle*. But they do, because ultimately, it's such a beautiful story. Louis B. Hobson writes in the *Calgary Sun*:

"If it were possible for a playwright posthumously to thank a company, surely Bertolt Brecht would stand up and applaud what Caravan Theatre has done with his *Caucasian Chalk Circle*.
Director Nick Hutchinson and the Caravan company have created a thoroughly entertaining evening of theatre without compromising the guidelines of Brecht's Marxist political and dramatic philosophies. Politically, Brecht slashed out at the bourgeois and dramatically he tried

Chalk Circle

to create an atmosphere that would prevent audiences from becoming too involved in the action of the play or identifying with the characters. Caravan Theatre's *Chalk Circle* is like a marvellous outdoor three-ring circus. Spotlights follow the actors and the action of the play as it travels from the centre circle through and around the audience. Sometimes the actors appear in masks, grotesque costumes or as troubadours. Even the most realistic of the characters sometimes breaks into song or becomes involved in slapstick shenanigans . . . in the second act the attention sways from Grusha to Azdak, the town drunk who becomes the country's legal mastermind. Hutchinson took over this role for the Alberta tour, and he proves himself as exciting and innovative an actor as he is a director. His Azdak is a flamboyant, loveable clown and a commanding stage personality . . . If the weather will co-operate in Calgary these next five days, Caravan Theatre will be able to thrill Calgarians with a unique and totally satisfying evening of pure theatrics."

We ended up on the outskirts of Calgary in a kind of wasteland not easily accessible to audiences, and our audience numbers dropped. The thing about travelling on the Caravan was that you girded your loins for the tour, and you looked forward to it, and it was exciting, and there were so many unexpected things that happened, and you never stopped working. Ever. At about two-thirds of the way through, you started counting the days when you could just have a morning where nothing happened, and you could cook your own breakfast, and you didn't see all those people that you saw every day.

N

ARTHUR

FERGUS

BRAMPTON

TORONTO

CLINTON

MITCHELL

STRATFORD

KITCHENER

Lake Ontario

STONEY CR.

NIAGARA ON THE LAKE

ANCASTER

BRANTFORD

GRIMSBY

BEAMSVILLE

ST. CATHARINES

HORSEPLAY
1981
ONTARIO

CHAPTER 16

Horseplay

Meanwhile, Peter Anderson and Phil Savath had been slogging away at what was going to be the next year's play, *Horseplay*. After the tour, we had a reading of where they'd got to and, "Whoopee! This is good!" Not only apt for us because of the geriatric horse characters Chevy, Ford, Dodge, Lincoln, and Rambler, but it was fun. It was a farce. It could play anywhere.

In fact, it was going to play Toronto because taking the show to Ontario was Paul Kirby's next grand step—a much bigger enterprise than hopping off to Alberta. Paul and Nans and Molly and I lived through the winter on the farm. A lot was involved in replacing our dead horses. Paul always managed to raise some extra money, though never enough, and horses came: a well-bred stallion, Laddie; Jenny, a Marilyn Monroe of Clyde mares; a bony old brood mare called Phyllis who we wondered how in hell we would keep alive because she was so skinny, and three more geldings for the road. Paul, with his impeccable hustle, had persuaded Dodge Inc. to give us a dual-wheel, three-quarter-ton pick-up truck for free, to trailer our light horses. To our amazement, the truck was actually delivered to the Salmon Arm dealership all the way from Ontario. Suzanne Morgan, Phil Savath, and Peter Anderson (our Chevy, Dodge, and Ford in the play) dressed up in their smartest gear, wearing the wonderful horse heads/masks that Melody Anderson had just

Our horses go to pick up the Dodge Ram dressed in their best

The brand new Cosmodrome

finished building. And they went off to Salmon Arm to receive the truck. The guy at the dealership didn't know what to do. He had to phone central office because he couldn't believe what was happening. So anyway, this fateful red truck (which will play a large part in stories of the Caravan to come) arrived at the farm amidst wild celebrations.

Then, Paul designed "The Cosmodrome," to which I objected hugely. The Cosmodrome was the rain cover, because we had lost money at different times with rain. It was going to cover the entire circle, which usually had wagons dotted around and then banners in between and a big entrance. For The Cosmodrome, you had six mega poles that had to be guyed into really strong stakes in the ground and then the poles connected to this thin fabric. It was beautiful, and it floated over the whole thing. But it doubled the set-up time, doubled what we had to carry, and it required another wagon and another team. And it took away the sky. It also had limited results when it rained; it helped in light rains but in heavy rains you couldn't hear a thing. It's the old story. What do you do when it's raining? And ultimately that leads you into a closed-in space. For me, the beauty of an open-air theatre is that it's an open-air theatre. If it rains, well, shit, it's too fucking bad. And you always find a solution of some kind.

Anyway, we had started with four wagons, and now were up to seven.

The music of *Horseplay*—which was directed by Doug Dodds (*Net City*), composed by Derek Hawksley, with lyrics by Peter Anderson and Phil Savath—gave us an enduring repertoire of horse anthems. Molly and I were going to go to Ontario to see the show up, and then we were coming back to work on our house and finally take time for ourselves.

The Caravan playing in Toronto

The tour began and it quickly became a slog. We weren't used to large populations and towns sometimes less than a day's travel apart, so the number of shows went up. And each time you've got to raise The Cosmodrome.

We made our way to Niagara-on-the-Lake, another theatre festival town. At the show, I stood behind Christopher Newton (formerly artistic director of the Vancouver Playhouse and now AD of the Shaw Festival) and his friends. They adored it. They had their minds blown, which was pretty gratifying: "My God, they're . . . Wow! Did you see?. . . Woo!!" That was an affirmation, coming from Christopher, and the show was really good. The Caravan was measuring up. Later in the tour, when we were trying to cover our deficits, John Hirsch, the distinguished Artistic Director of The Stratford Shakespearean Festival, wrote the following to the Ontario Minister of Culture:

> "I wish to write on behalf of the Caravan Stage Co and the NDWT group. Recently this group came to perform their Horse Show at Stratford, and I had a chance to see the kind of theatre which I consider to be a very vital and essential part of our theatre ecology. The performers are all highly skilled professionals who because of the format of their theatre are able to bring performances to places throughout Ontario where live theatre would otherwise not be seen. In their work, the people at Caravan Stage continue the tradition of performance from which other more permanent theatres can learn a great deal about working with diverse audiences, about improvisation, and dedication to the profession. In watching the reactions of the audiences, I saw pure enjoyment, attention, and true appreciation of the artists efforts."

Chevy (Suzanne Morgan), Dodge (Phil Savath), Ford (Peter Anderson), Lincoln (Ross Imrie)
Photo & Masks by Melody Anderson

Molly, Nick and March at home on the farm

Molly and I came back to the farm. We were building our house backwards because it had a square upper floor set in an octagonal lower floor. I figured that building a square was hard enough, let alone building on an octagon, if you've never built anything before. So, we started doing that and the building inspector came, and he had a conniption and left saying, "Desist on this building immediately, until you have proper bracing." So, I hammered on some rudimentary bracing and, fortunately, he never came back. I think he didn't wanted to know. Once the upper floor and roof were done, we had a bedroom and a ladder to climb up. Even Coyote, the dog, could climb it.

The Ontario tour had put the Caravan squarely on a new map, but our sponsor NDWT (Ne'er Do Well Thespians), a cutting-edge theatre in Toronto under Keith Turnbull, was sunk. The show didn't meet the expected money. On the plus side, we inherited Catherine O'Grady, their administrator, who got together with one of our *Horseplay* horses, Ross Imrie, and they came back to reinforce the farm contingent.

Almost every exhausted Caravaner came off the tour saying, "That's it! Never again!" The transport trucks bearing the wagons wouldn't release the wagons until the trucking company was paid in full. So, Paul went down to our credit union, cornered the loans' manager, and after a long session and much difficulty they gave us a loan for twenty thousand, a fateful second mortgage. It got the wagons off the trucks but jeopardized a vital deal we had made on the first mortgage. Shortly after buying the farm, we had negotiated an agreement with the Tides Foundation (set up to encourage land stewardship) which stated that when we had set covenants protecting the farm, in event of future sales, the Foundation would forgive the first mortgage that they held. But you couldn't retire a first mortgage until you retired a second and the second has pride of place in the line-up of everything, so this caused mass consternation.

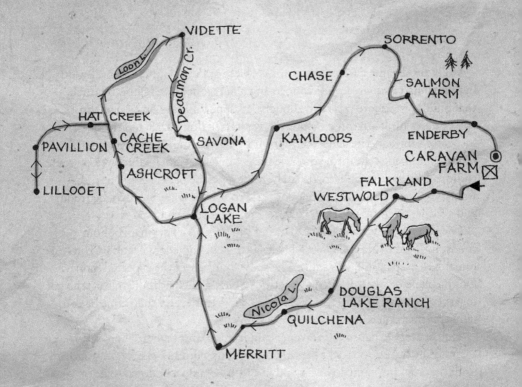

LAW OF
THE LAND
1982

CHAPTER 17

Law of the Land

That winter, a theatre company in Nelson asked me to direct *The Threepenny Opera,* and I met Corky, and Bonnie Evans who were going to billet Molly and me. They were both committed political activists, and we became firm friends. It was in their home that our daughter March was conceived. So now the deadline for completing our house on the farm was nine months away—October.

When we got back to the farm, it was spring. There was no snow on the ground. Paul came to have a meeting with Molly and me about the next show, for which no one wanted to go back on the road:

"I've got this idea for the next tour. We're gonna leave the wagons behind, pack the horses and go overland, off the road, just like you always wanted to. And we're gonna go to Hat Creek and Lillooet.

Whadya say?"

"Oh, Paul, you couldn't've thought of anything we'd like more to do. Wonderful! We're in!"

I didn't want to direct, but I'd act. And Keith Turnbull, from the now defunct NDWT in Toronto, wanted to direct even if the Caravan had sunk his theatre. The play was targeting an open-pit coal mine project destined for the area where we were touring, which had already become a serious controversy. Peter Anderson, Keith, and I were putting the finishing touches on Peter's script *Law of the Land* when I broached the issue of the set, since we were going overland with packhorses. Keith said, "What?! You're going to take away all the toys?" So back came the wagons.

The rewrites had cost us a week of rehearsal, but Keith kept his cool. He is a super hands-off director; he lets things happen and then sorts them out. He's the opposite of me. And I was very frustrated when I started working on the lead role of Coyote because he refused to tell me what to do. But maybe that process worked, and I had a really good time playing the part.

It was a very "off the main road" tour even though we weren't pack-horsing it. I had two terrifying runaways. I was bowling across the Douglas Lake Ranch in the pub bug with two ten-year-olds, Darcy and Sergeo (Paul and Nan's middle son). I was driving Clyde—the old partner of my first runaway horse, Dale—not a care in the world, no traffic, open country, when, "Ahh!!

Darcy Hutchinson and Peter Anderson on tour with Law of the land

Oh no, a white rock!" And the horse goes *zzzooooooom* off the road, turns a hard right and I'm flung off the wagon. And then the wagon goes round in a circle, back over the road, down into the bush, and hits a log, which stops it. And the kids are still in it, dazed. It was brutal. The wheel needed fixing. So yet again, the advance wagon had to wait while the rest passed it. A couple of days later we caught them up, in the most mosquito-infested spot I've ever seen. We were greeted by the company all swathed in scarves and blankets. The scene looked as if it came straight out of *Lawrence of Arabia*.

When we arrived in Ashcroft, the hottest place in British Columbia, and were ready to do the show, there were fewer people in the audience than in the company. So, the question was raised, "Do we do the show?" We put it to a vote and the majority was for cancelling. Everyone slunk away, and five minutes later returned to reverse their decision—true Caravan democracy in action.

Runaway number four happens on the way to Lillooet, the furthest westerly point on our tour and of course well known to me as the end of our horse adventure into the Chilcotin, years before. Young Linz Kenyon, who was playing guitar on his father's porch when I first got Snake, is on his first Caravan tour. He's my shotgun and Molly is outrider. The Gold Rush Festival in Lillooet has just finished. A camel mounted on wheels, left over

The cast of Law of the land

from the parade, is parked by the side of the road. I remember the antipathy between horses and camels, so I wind my lines round my hands, since good old Clyde has already proved to be a runaway and if ever there's going to be a runaway, this may be it. Molly is on her toes, and she's riding between us and the camel. And we make it past the camel. We're exhausted, and right on the corner there's a diner and we are starving. So, we pull in. Phew! We get a break. We're in a hurry to unhook. Linz goes to one side of the horse and I the other, and we're unhooking the chains that connect the horse to the wagon. In that very moment, a car slows down and then accelerates and *BOOM! BANG!*—a backfire. Well, the horse hasn't been properly unhooked and there is nobody at his head and he's down the main street at a formidable gallop with all our stuff flying out of the wagon. I stop the first car that comes along, open the door, jump in, and say, "Go after that wagon, *please!*" There are four good old native boys in that car: "Ho, I see. He's travellin' real good. Okay. Come on, Sam, let's go." And we accelerate to twenty-five miles an hour and go after the horse. At which point, Clyde suddenly decides to leave the road. He goes down an almost impossibly steep embankment which leads to the railroad tracks at the bottom. He bounces over one set of tracks, wagon and all, and then hits the next set of tracks and one of the wheels breaks. End of runaway number four.

Our shows in the Lillooet/Hat Creek area, the site of the proposed coal mine, were largely popular and brought out all the bushwhacked, politico hippies from near and far. My favourite moment of all: just as the show was starting in Lillooet, a majestic cowboy on horseback appeared. It was Harry Kenyon, Snake's old owner, who had ridden apparently miles from his home in the D'Arcy Valley to see his son Linz in the show. How romantic was that! Until we discovered that Harry had trailered his horse behind his camper and was parked just around the corner!

Throughout the return journey, pregnant Molly was getting bigger and bigger; day by day she was shedding more and more of the padding originally stitched into her costumes for the Japanese businessman and "deer" she was playing in the show. In Salmon Arm, my dad Jeremy and his wife June arrived. A great occasion, as this was the first time my dad had come out west or seen me in a show.

June wrote to Peggy:
"Before we set off for the farm, I must scribble you a line about the show. First and foremost, to say that Nick was terrific. I know I'm not an expert but to me it simply was an unforgettable performance. As you know he plays a coyote (wolf) who changes himself into an old cowboy and then back again into a coyote. In both, he was quite amazing. As the animal he seemed to be charged with an almost electrical vitality which pervaded the entire auditorium and then suddenly he became the old, battered Cowboy of the Wild West and honestly, he looked and moved like a seventy year old!!! . . . I won't go into too much detail about the show . . . but just to say Darcy was irresistible in it. Perched sky-high he was a crow in homburg and black tailcoat, tiny black beak and large tennis shoes and whistle completed the picture. He sat perched throughout, looking rather sleepy in the searchlights, but oh my when his lines came, including ones like metaphysical and pollutionisation, he fairly delivered them in true Ashcroftian style! Molly was extraordinary too—she leapt and cavorted about like a small child instead of practically a mother. Jeremy and I both found the whole show marvelous and they played to their largest ever audience—five hundred."

To which Jeremy added:
"I feel so much much happier about Nick and the future and of course it's all fraught and always will be, but that's really the point. Nick's euphoria on getting back to the peace and quiet of the country was so fundamental—he really does hate the towns and traffic."

We were back at the farm in September, and the baby was due in October, so it was fix up the house. Molly wanted to put a hand pump on the well. I said, "Molly, no. We're going to have running water or I'll die. You'll die too." I got a holding tank above the house readied and connected so that we could pump water from the well up into it and then gravity-feed it back to the house. It was finally working just before Molly went into hospital. (Except that I hadn't covered in the pipes which, of course, froze in the fall weather.) And March was born.

Nick and March at breakfast

CHAPTER 18

The Last Wild Horse

In the spring, I was invited back to the National Theatre School in Montreal by Michael Mawson and Perry Schneiderman, who were now running things. I directed an exciting production of Poliakoff's *Strawberry Fields*.

Meanwhile, back at the farm, Sharon Stearns and George Ryga were developing the script that would eventually become *Wagons and Dragons* for the Caravan's 1983 tour. Just before the beginning of rehearsals, Molly and I were visited at our house by Paul who, along with Nans, wanted to be recast in more major parts. He argued that having devoted all this time to building the company, surely they should be given lead roles: "I don't want to go on doing this job, if all I'm doing is tiny parts." What could I say? Paul had never had the lead, but he'd had plenty of chunky parts. Nans as well. And Paul was forever, and rightly so, on the phone, in and out of the office, running the company as only he knew how. But now there was sign of a fissure.

Wagons and Dragons was partly an experiment in taking the wagons through the audience. You wouldn't do it nowadays. Little children sitting with a rope-marked runway and these huge horses clip-clopping by, pulling these huge wagons. The thought of it still terrifies me, but no one was hurt. It wasn't a happy show. It was a smaller cast and had little of the Caravan magic.

That spring, Catherine Hahn had come back from spending time with Bread and Puppet Theatre in Vermont and had this notion of a horse pageant. A one-off event on the farm. We all got behind it. We could do it on the farm while the tours were on. Or at the end of the tour. Paul was dead set against it. We have endless discussions. The fissure is widening.

Despite Paul and Nans' resistance, we went ahead with *The Last Wild Horse*. It was a moment of complete liberation of all constraints and an exploration of pageantry and image. It wasn't really directed.

Catherine conceptualized it and everybody's imagination took off in whatever direction they wanted. Led by a triumphant brass band, the audience arrived behind a Clyde mare giving birth to the "last wild horse" and a dancer swathed in saranwrap emerged from the mare's hind legs . . . the four horsemen of the apocalypse came streaking across a field. There was virtually no text. I was Don Coyote up in a tree declaring, "God damn is mad dog spelled backwards," at which point all our Mennonite neighbours got to their feet

Nick riding Rocinante pushed by Darcy

and left. I slid down on a cable and boarded our beautiful Clydesdale stallion and rode off into the distance. Back I came into the riding ring on Rocinante, a huge horse that I had built out of old, dead wood, seemingly pushed by my eleven-year-old son Darcy, but actually pulled by a cable. I belted out some fabulous speech and jousted with a monster, which, when I killed it, broke open and helium balloons carried the spirit of the last wild horse into the air and over the mountains while Rocinante burst into flames. Then eight wagons from all our different teamster friends arrived at the riding ring, picked up the whole audience and took them down the hill to where Derek's gypsy band was playing around a huge campfire. It established the farm as a performance space and the Farm Theatre was born. The fissure got bigger.

That spring, I returned to NTS and directed Edward Bond's Restoration, taking it to Harbourfront in Toronto. It was a great success; I would put it very near the top of any of the shows I've done. Back at the farm, the company is rehearsing Richard Pochenko's version of Hands Up! on their way to California for a three-year tour. Kirby is never unambitious. They "Jal the Drom" and off they go—leaving Molly, March, me, Catherine, Ross, Paul White, and Paul Kirkwood Hackett on the farm. They get as far as Vernon, and Paul and Nans invite Molly and me to join them for dinner in some restaurant. Sitting around a table, the bombshell drops. They aren't ever coming back to the farm: the farm gobbles up money faster than the show—it is unsustainable . . . and if cutting off the farm is essential to keeping the Caravan Stage Company, then so be it. In hindsight, it was easy to see the signs. But in the moment, we are gobsmacked.

It would take time for all the repercussions to surface. The first of those was how to put food on the table—because they got the money, honey. They had the Canada Council grant, which was our financial bedrock. At least Paul had put in place a board of directors that was independent of the members of the company. Previously, any decisions relating to the Bill Miner Society (that is, the non-profit society responsible for all things financial) had been made by a quorum of Caravaners at highly informal annual meetings. The new board would be responsible for all the assets of the Caravan—but, in reality, only those assets left at the farm. Was Paul's expectation that those left at the farm would fold up their tents and the farm would be sold? One of the farm's major expenses was still the second mortgage.

The one asset we did have was horses. Some would have to be sold. We also had the famous red Dodge dual-wheeled pick-up donated for the tour in Ontario. The problem with it was it ate up gas, and Paul had scored, for next to nothing, a monster diesel motor that he'd managed to talk Paul White into installing. Paul White had spent the better part of two years switching out the motors on the Dodge. At this point, it was just about ready to make its virgin run to the grand draft-horse auction in Idaho, where we were reluctantly sending four of our horses. Paul White and I set off trailering the four Clydes (approximately four tons worth), to discover that we could only make about twenty miles an hour whenever we hit an uphill grade. And to get to Idaho, you have to cross a number of mountain passes, which we did at close to walking speed. But we got there and sold the horses and came back with a whack of dough. Subsequently, Paul had to switch out the engines once more, rewire the original and sell the truck to recover his costs. It was one of those endless Sisyphean tasks!

Of course, the seven of us of us left on the farm were not gonna fold up camp and leave. It was the first real chance to put our energies to work the farm. Ross and I worked the fields with the horses that were left, mainly plowing and preparing for future spring crops as well as haying. And thanks to Molly we had lots of vegetables. Our motto became "Art and Potatoes." To keep our oar in on the arts' side, I secured some money from the Canada Council (who were, of course, a bit worried about the "separation") for a directors' workshop exploring *Fool for Love* by Sam Shepherd. The workshop involved six young directors, with Peter Anderson, Wendy Van Riesen, and me as actors, working with Molly and Catherine as designers. By the end of that summer, when the enormity of the upheaval had sunk in, we knew we could work a farm, put on a show à la *Last Wild Horse* and do workshops. But of coarse, penury persisted.

In the fall, Montreal was calling again. Maurice Podbury of the Centaur Theatre asked me to do a production of *Marivaux's' L'Heureux Stratagème, Successful Strategies*. In a letter to Maurice, the great Jean Louis Barrault congratulated The Centaur on reviving Marivaux:

> "Sensual, refined, perverted and yet, in spite of all, full of good sense. Marivaux has the cruelty of the Sadist, the tough materialism of the Bourgeois, the elegance of the aristocrat, the indignation of the revolutionary and the comic wisdom of the spirit of the people."

Martha Burns, Corrine Koslo and Paul Cross in Successful Strategies

What more could you want?! I was getting pressure to be the artistic director of the English section of N.T.S. which increased with the success of the Centaur production. Given the events at the farm, it didn't appear to be a realistic option. On my return to the farm, we decided to do a production of *George Orwell's Animal Farm*. We proposed it successfully to the Canada Council for the Arts as a project grant, since we had no operating funding, and we set Peter Anderson to work on an adaptation. For the purposes of funding, we had to argue that theatre at the Caravan Farm had validity. And therefore, in the early summer, Molly and I and two members of the Canada Council travelled to San Francisco to meet with Paul and Nans to discuss funding. Out of this prickly negotiation an agreement was reached, whereby we would receive thirty percent of the operating grant and the Caravan Stage Company would receive seventy per cent.

Scenes from Animal Farm

The company for Animal Farm, was approximately one-half Caravan veterans and one-half members of our local community. It was performed promenade style (the audience stands and walks) round the farmyard itself. The animal characters were masked beautifully by Catherine Hahn. For the first scene, played in front of the four wagon bays in the new wagon shed, we built seating to accommodate approximately two hundred people. By the end of the six shows, we were playing to seven hundred people. The beauty of the audience response was that so many who had seen the Stage Company on the road came for the first time to the farm. The Caravan Farm Theatre was on the map. This was the summer of 1985.

As I already mentioned, the pressure to run the English Section of the NTS was mounting. I couldn't leave the farm, and I couldn't leave Molly and March. It was too much. But it was nevertheless tempting— returning to teaching, real resources, and opening new horizons—but I insisted, "No, this is impossible." Then Perry Schneiderman and Michael Mawson, who had brought me back recently as a guest director, called me up: "Hey Nick, we realize you're busy as hell at the Caravan, but we need you. We need your bright, shiny, weather-beaten face to give our organization a little glamour. How about we share the direction between the three of us?" I went to Montreal to discuss, and the ball went around and around and around. Michael proposed the university pattern of "chairs" that switch yearly. I remembered the old cowboy on the trail who had spat out, "Three's no good!" and said, "Sorry, guys, I'm going in by myself." The selection committee was made up of a number of my old teachers, including Pierre Lefèvre, so I got the job.

Molly wasn't very keen on the idea for the very same reasons that I wasn't, so it was a bit of a life-changing decision. It had real plusses— like, for instance, a salary! After however many years at the Caravan, to actually be paid a salary, to get all those things like retirement and dental . . . After Caravan wages, it seemed like a huge amount of money although it was, in fact, a pretty poorly paid job. But most importantly, it was the chance to re-explore theatre training and reconnect with all that had influenced my journey in the theatre. I was also pretty excited about possibly working again in French and English. I really didn't know how things were between the English and the French sections of the school. It wasn't very good. We were at the beginning of the eighties, the Parti Québécois had passed Bill 101 in 1977, a French-language bill which prioritised French language in all aspects of Québécois life. It was not popular with the Anglo population and there was a real standoffishness from the Québécois to the English and vice-versa.

The French side of the school is a vibrant part of the Québécois culture— teachers and students have a culture in common—whereas the English section is drawn from all parts of Canada to a city where they don't speak the language.

The founding fathers of the school had intended that training would take place partly in Montreal and partly at Stratford with a view to a permanent cultural exchange. This never happened, and to this day there is a strong voice arguing that the English section should be moved to Toronto. What a classic Canadian conundrum.

Anyway, here I go:

- Audition Tour
- Travel Planning
- Three sets of Curricula and Finding teachers
- Casting the students
- Interact at the administration level with the Design Section, the Tech Section, the Administration, the French Section
- And of course, not forgetting next summer's planning for the newly emerging Caravan Farm Theatre

It leaves a person breathless. But the little time allotted to actually teach and direct is precious.

CHAPTER 19

As You Like It

Coming at a gallop, post audition tour and selection of new students, it was back to the farm for next summer's *As You Like It*.

Shakespeare had been hovering for a while. It was too much for the road, and it was risky, and you had to have people who could handle it. But on the farm, the obvious choices were *As You Like It* or *A Midsummer Night's Dream*—they both take place in the woods. The dynamic of the court and exile in the forest, which is at the heart of As You Like It, made it a very relevant choice for the second farm production:

Now my Coe-mates, and brothers in exile:
Hath not old custome made this life more sweete
Than that of painted pompe?Are not these woods
More free from peril than the envious Court?
Heere feele we not the penaltie of Adam,
The seasons difference as the Icie phange
And churlish chiding of the winters winde,
Which when it bites and blowes upon my body
Even till I shrinke with cold, I smile and say
This is no flattery: these are counsellors
That feelingly perswade me what I am:
Sweete are the uses of adversitie
Which like the toad, ougly and venomous,
Weares yet a precious Jewell in his head:
And this our life exempt from publicke haunt,
Findes tongues in trees, bookes in the running brookes,
Sermons in stones, and good in every thing

As You Like It, Act2 Sc1

That was the good duke. My speech. The bad duke, whose coup d'état had exiled the good duke, was played by Keith Turnbull, who co-directed with me. Having both directors performing and directing each other's scenes was a fascinating dynamic. We'd both had recent revelations about Shakespeare text

Keith Turnbull and Nick. Co-directors of As You like It

in the original First Folio editions. (All the Shakespeare quotes in this book use the First Folio text.) The spelling is different, as is the punctuation and capitalisation. It is text for speaking and provides the actor with innumerable clues. We had built a gazebo performance space as the perfect place for the court; when the play moved to the Forest of Arden, we would move the audience into our forest. But, of course, that became impossibly cumbersome for what needs to be a fast-moving scene-to-scene unfolding of the story.

And like so many preconceived ideas, it had to be abandoned. After all, "All the world's a stage." And the gazebo was a beauty. At this point in time, we had no practical seating, as *Animal Farm* had been done "promenade," so five bleachers were built to surround the gazebo stage despite the protestations of our new board of directors who couldn't see where the money would come from.

It was a rainy summer, and we lost a few shows. People were coming, but not in the droves that had come to *Animal Farm*, which was chastening. But on the other hand, I think it elevated our work because Shakespeare always does. And it also elevates the audience. If you get the words across, the audience has a whole new tuning and magic happens. Walking back towards the performance one evening after a light sprinkle of rain, the voices and words coming from the stage were breathtakingly clear and it finally sank in that sound is carried by moisture just as it is impeded by dry heat. Lessons that only outdoor theatre will teach. We had a few peacocks on the farm and they would frequently punctuate high emotional moments with their cries. One night, the courtier Le Beau took his ostentatious entrance all the way around the gazebo with his tailcoat decorated in peacock feathers . . . followed all the way by a strutting peacock!

Annie Skinner, one of the great Canadian voice teachers, with whom I had collaborated before, was there when I started at the School. Perry Schneiderman, who knew the administrative mechanics, pulled me out of deep water every time I looked like I was sinking. My old teacher Pierre Lefèvre would come and give eight weeks of master classes in mask with the first and second years, and his work was a lynch pin as it had always been in Strasbourg. My favourite times were working with the students directly.

It was the end of term, graduation, and Molly and March had gone back to the farm early. I got a phone call that Molly had had a serious accident coming off a horse and ruptured her spleen. We had worked with horses now for a number of years without serious incident, but this time it was a matter life and death, which is unfortunately almost inevitable the longer you work with horses. So, taking my medical encyclopedia with me to explain what the spleen was and what it did, I flew back. Molly was in intensive care at our local hospital. Her mum had arrived to look after four-year-old March. It was an agonising few days, dealing with hospital, doctors, staying in a seedy motel to be near Molly. The big question was whether they would remove the spleen, which was the conventional treatment. Received wisdom was, "Oh the spleen is really not that important—like the appendix or adenoids you can get by quite well without it." Molly and I were not convinced of this and pestered the doctors. By a near miracle, and to our undying gratitude, the doctors managed to save her spleen by wrapping it in an amazing fabric that kept it intact. And after a few days, we very gingerly brought Molly back to the farm. In Chinese medicine, the spleen is the mother organ regulating all the others. I mentioned earlier how reluctant Molly was about the Montreal reality and how she felt about leaving the farm. Most of her life had been one of constant of moving and the farm was the place she had finally put down roots. On top which, it was hard for March, at the age of four, to cope with the back and forth. The accident exposed this fault line in our relationship.

The pressure was off at the beginning of summer because we were remounting *As You Like It* and it went smoothly. Peter Anderson had been working on *Bull by the Horns*, a completely hilarious pastiche-Western. We took it away from the gazebo and put it in the riding ring. It had a huge broad set of a false-fronted Western town with the audience bleachers all in a straight line looking at it in Cinemascope. The show begins: a tumbleweed rolls through the empty town and Peter— as the hero, Rattlesnake Smith—jumps up as he is being bitten by a rattlesnake. It was a big hit. Good weather, sold out audiences.

Everything on the farm was powered from a somewhat inadequate electric service down in the cook shack. For *Bull by the Horns*, we ran all our lighting cables half a click away to the riding ring. Our fabulous lighting mistress, Bev Peacock, had forbidden toast-making during the show; despite this, someone popped a slice into the toaster and all the fuses blew. In the middle of the show, we were all in the dark. Our local electrical inspector just happened to be in the audience that night. There must've been a full moon because he was seen rising to his feet and disappearing as quickly as he could. It was too late and too dark for him to fulfill his role. I called him the next day, and he said:

Jan Kudelka with the cast of Bull by the Horns

"You'll need an electrical contractor." "Well, who do you think I should get?"
"I can't tell you."

I had the yellow pages of electrical contractors and started reading him off
the names. Somehow, with a breathy grunt, he gave me a very subtle indication
of who suited us best. A lovely wall-eyed electrician arrived the next day with
the inspector. As they climbed up the hill from the cook shack, they stopped at
each connection. The inspector would say:

"Well Jim, what do you think of that?" And Jim with his wall-eye would say:
"Well, that's different."

They did that the whole way up to the show site. And then we had to spend
most of our hard-earned profits on a major cable and substation for the power.
Infrastructure. Little by little.

Back to the school for the fall term, the pressure was beginning to build on
all fronts as to what to do next. Which director should direct which play for the
third years? What should the second year third slot be? Who should we get to
teach the main acting course in the first year because so-and-so wasn't available?
And most importantly, what was the next summer show at the Caravan?

Molly, March, Darcy and I went off to the Bahamas on one of those cheapo
excursions with a not-very-nice hotel. The weather was lousy so there was no
beach. I was in a funk with all the decisions, but finally came up for air and
figured we should do our version of Brecht's *The Good Woman of Szechuan*,

adapting it into *The Good Woman of Saskatchewan*, replacing Brecht's tobacco factory with liquor and the Prohibition era.

That summer, near the end of rehearsal, I again had to "disappear." I hadn't done that since I bolted from Strasbourg. But I got to a place in rehearsal where I didn't know how to fix things and couldn't see a way to make anything work. Everything just got blacker. I was entering into the depressive state. There's a point when you get to the run-through phase of rehearsal, where your notes to the cast are either creative or negative. You know: "Don't do this. Cut this. Why are you doing this?" The negative. And the other is: "Wow! Do see what happened? You're making me understand what this part of the play is about." A good session can be spellbinding. And everybody wants more. They want you to tell them how they were. That's what an actor wants. When you're "weary, feeling small," you've got very little to say to any cast, and inevitably shame comes into the picture. I disappear, back to our house. Of course, everybody gets concerned and sorts everything out on their own! I manage to creep back in time for the last rehearsals and the show works perfectly well, which just underlines the fact that in mental illness everything is ultimately subjective and judgement is skewed. Looking back, it's pretty obvious I was starting to burn out.

Well before the Caravan Stage Company left the farm forever, we had begun to give horse-drawn sleigh rides in the snowy season for small-scale parties, Christmas events, etc. It was a great way to give the idle horses work and keep them fit in the winter, and little by little the demand for the rides increased. Shortly after the Stage Company left, and when revenues were of paramount importance, they became one of the more serious income producers for the farm.

One evening had been entirely booked by the RCMP constabulary of Armstrong, who were led by a very genial cop known as Pete the Heat. Given that this was a full evening booking, we figured we had to prepare some extraordinary measures for their ride. Molly was driving, and David Balser and I prepared our bandito costumes and galloped across the back-forty, bandana-ed, to hold up the sleigh. We roped them in and charged them with "drunk and disorderly conduct." We slipped a bag of green leaf into Pete the Heat's pocket and then made much of its discovery. They all had a good laugh. Those were the days when the police had a good sense of humour; there was great merriment as they trotted at full tilt back to the cook shack, where the serious drinking began. They left the farm at three a.m.

Perhaps that was the seed for the "sleigh-ride theatre" that was to evolve. Following the *Good Woman of Saskatchewan*, Peter Hall came up with a proposal for a winter show using the sleighs to transport the audience to a Christmas story, *The Coming of the Kings*, by Ted Hughes. The show played to packed slieghs and it became clear that a show during the Christmas/New Year time would have substantial appeal and garner real income.

Most importantly, it provided the horses with a serious function now that they were no longer travelling on the road. Four teams of horses pulled the four sleighs. Year by year, the sleigh-ride shows developed from being merely a transport of audience to a stage somewhere on the farm, to becoming more and more integrated into the storytelling. From one show a night, demand was such that we increased to three.

The second sleigh-ride show was *The Nativity*, written by Peter Anderson who had been at work on a *Mystery Cycle* for the farm. *The Mystery Cycles* were a medieval community telling of the Bible in street theatre format, where each section of that story was taken on by a guild (a brotherhood of skilled workers, carpenters, builders, cooks etc.). It was truly a community event. Both Molly and I were very taken with the Eugenio Barba dictum "every seven years, a volcano"—throw it all up, see where it lands, and go on to the next. In London I had seen the first part of the National Theatre's *Mystery Cycle*, and it had opened a door for me to seeing the myths of the Bible as stories that related to one's own reality. The volcanic energy of confronting the religious stories, rejected in large part by our generation, seemed to be the seven-year volcano Barba talked about. The structure of our cycles would be three plays: *Creation, The Nativity, and The Passion.*

The Kids from Romeo and Juliet

It's 1989—summer at the farm and the first night of *Romeo and Juliet*. A few minutes before the half hour, I'm walking through the yard and I suddenly think, This doesn't feel like a first night. There's something weird. There's no hustle and scuffle and bustle and tearing about in crisis. It's calm. And I make my way up to the gazebo and nothing's really happening, people haven't quite got to places, and the audience is just coming in. I turn around and the sky has turned copper. A light shaded copper. And then, pinching myself, I behold two rainbows— vertical, not joining, going up parallel to each other so that they frame the hill we are on. Whoooa! And then everything starts just fine. Everything is quiet and beautiful, good audience and everything. The scene gets to where the boys, Mercutio and Romeo and their gang, are going to crash the Capulet party, carrying their kerosene torches.

Mercutio starts the Queen Mab speech: "She is the fairy's midwife and she comes in shape no bigger than an agate stone pricked on the lazy finger of a maid." And the torches suddenly go Psheeeeew! Horizontal. The wind has just started to blow. It doesn't quite blow the torches out but it's blowing into the big party. The stage is filling up with all the guests. Here's Romeo and there's Juliet at opposite ends of the earth, and when they turn and have that fateful look, the loudest crack of thunder you have ever heard in your life CRRRRRRACKS! And the skies open and drench, in one fell drench, the entire space. And I've jumped up and I'm calling the audience onto the stage because that's the only shelter. So, then we have a hundred and fifty people squeezed together on the gazebo stage singing, "Swing Low, Sweet Chariot," while this raging torrent of water is pulsating down. Costumes are sailing down towards the cook shack or the wagon shed where light bulbs have been blown out of their sockets . . . and that's the end of opening night of *Romeo and Juliet*.

That's what you get for doing outdoor theatre. How Nature can reflect on what you do. So what if the audience has only seen half the play? They've had an unforgettable experience. But there's always a price to pay and sooner or later, like the Stage Company's cosmodrome, we have to protect ourselves from rain and we resolve to find a circus tent. Oh, the art of compromise! I'm not very good at it.

But ultimately a rain tent had to be had and for the next two summers, we lost the sky—and of course it never really rained!

To my great surprise—because momentous decisions in my life are rarely made with much forethought—somewhere in the first half of my fourth year at NTS I pulled the plug and quit. It was basically burn-out and a couple of tablespoons of frustration. Montreal life was not easy for Molly and she missed the farm, as did I.

But I also fundamentally believed that if one wanted a school which was run by active theatre artists, four or five years was enough.

CHAPTER 20

Peggy's last visit

1990. The goodbye year in Montreal turned out to be, ironically, the most rewarding of my tenure. I did a King Lear second year exercise that had Pierre Lefèvre pouring tears. Rarely have I ever seen a second year group of students handle such a supremely challenging Shakespeare with such passion, clarity, and deep understanding. It was an exceptional group. My final production with the graduating class was a double bill of a Feydeau, always a gas, and an Edward Bond opera, *The Cat*, that went on tour across the country where, in Edmonton, I said a poignant farewell to their company.

In addition, I had been approached by Vincent de Tourdonnet, who was working on a musical with Allen Cole inspired from Jules Romain's *Knock, ou le triomphe de la Medicine*, the most recent in a tradition of French plays satirizing the impostors of the medical profession. Their adaptation, *Strange Medicine*, was slated for production that summer. In Montreal we gathered a few potential cast members for a workshop.

For the first time, the aforementioned circus tent went up. And of course, it never rained. It was the first Caravan full-blown through-scored operetta/musical. A great balance between professionals and community actors and in particular, kids! Two new arrivals at the farm, Jimmy Tait and Randi Helmers, led the company—and became long-term members. Meanwhile, Molly and Cathy Stubbington (a puppeteer she had got to know in Montreal) and a small group went out on the road again for the second year with a beautiful marionette show, *The Dragon's Forge*, which played out of the Sally wagon.

Strange Medicine is done, and well done, and I'm not going back to the school. Hallelujah! I'm a free man! But already my plate is almost indigestibly full. First the winter show, *The Snow Queen*, where the sleighs and their journeys cross the farm in a fast-moving sleigh-ride version of promenade theatre. It will be a long journey and a freezing cold winter. But much in the vein of *Animal Farm, The Snow Queen* magically reflects the farm. Two images remain in the memory: Gerda setting off on her quest for her brother Kai in a little boat pulled by the lead sleigh surrounded by the others, across the snow. And then our dear old teamster Ted, ex-chuckwagon racer, who loved high-speed adventure, tearing at full gallop over the hill with the Snow Queen herself (played by Jimmy Tait) standing on the back of his sleigh, and taking a corner too sharply, the whole rig capsizing—sending the queen in her flowing white robes skidding across the snow.

That was the first thing on the plate. Then there's the beginning of the creative process for *the Mystery Cycle*, the first part of which, *Creation*, is to be a co-production with Western Canada Theatre Company in Kamloops, in conjunction with the Kamloops Indian Band.

We've lined up seventy-six actors, musicians, designers, technicians, etc., who will be arriving in April and May. And so will my mother, Peggy, who has been nominated for an Oscar for A Passage to India (and wins it). Darcy, my now teenage son, and I are meant to accompany her to the event.

But first, Molly, March, Darcy, and I head out to stay with Molly's mother and father in Hawaii. On the plane, the news arrives that the U.S. has declared its first war on Iraq. Molly's Dad, Patrick, is a retired navy admiral who has dealt in his career with all matters pertaining to intelligence. To our great surprise, the news of the war has deeply angered him, and we decamp for our little holiday to the navy's recreational beach, where we find marines in full exercise mode. It makes for a certain level of tension in our little holiday house. Then comes the news that Peggy has a bit of a cold and has decided to cancel her appearance at the Oscars so that she can be in full form for her visit to the farm in a few months. Darcy and I discard our sumptuous Oscar wardrobes with a twinge of relief.

Over the past ten years, Peggy had had a major film and television career and had unloaded some of its ill-gotten gains on my sister and me. The neighbouring farm to the Caravan was coming up for sale and the neighbours real estate agent was vaunting its attributes. So, I bought it. It seemed a good investment—but most importantly it would provide more hay and pasture, barns, and outbuildings for the Caravan.

Peggy was to arrive in April, so Molly and I built a new room into the house at ground level and procured a brand new porta-potty. Peggy arrived and was delighted, like a little girl, with her new room and of course the porta-potty, because she had been dreading squatting over our very primitive "out-hole," which had served us for years.

She was eighty-three, but as always, full of energy, plans, and names. She would sit in the house, rapt in a thumb-twiddle, pondering appropriate names for whatever there was—in this case, she had decided to ponder what to call the new farm. One evening, when I came down from fixing a water pipe, she exclaimed:

"I've got it!" "Got what?"

"The farm. It's Freshwoods Farm."

"Maaa, that's kind of an awfully sugary name for what's a rather ugly farm. Don't you think "Tin Barn" would be better? And anyway, where does Freshwoods Farm come from?"

Nick and Peggy rehearsing for the Creation Workshop

"Oh, it's Browning, from Lycidas: 'At last he rose and donned his mantle blue, Anon to fresh woods and pastures new.'"

Her stay was joyful. We went driving around in the little stud cart visiting neighbours on the corner. She planted trees at the new farm, which was now available for occupation.

We were accumulating elements for the "Earth Orchestra," a project of Richard Owings, the musical director for the upcoming production of *Creation*. It was to be composed of found objects from the farm and recycled car parts from local junkyards and dumps. Don Waring, from *the Sound Symposium* in Newfoundland, was to lead the workshop, which ended with a reading of parts of the script to the sounds of the new orchestra. Peggy, wrapped up in shawls and scarves, sitting in the circle of crazy instruments, read Naomi's speech, forewarning the imminent flood in the story of Noah. She didn't do a bad job. Unbeknownst to anyone on or off the farm, this was to be her last performance.

On her last night, she resolved to cook a ham for the company. I had to intervene occasionally in the process because my mother was not exactly the most experienced of cooks. After some intervention or other, I must have made some ironic comment that drew her to her full five-foot-three height and her full-throated powerhouse of a voice exclaimed "FUCK OFF!" It resonated across the cook shack and everyone had a great laugh.

She left to stay the night in Vancouver with friends before taking the plane to London. She phoned in a panic to say she'd left her diary with everything in it somewhere. Could I look? "I think it might have been the cook shack," she said. I searched the cook shack and I found it under a bench. On the way to the phone, I rifled through it. There was nothing in the diary whatsoever, except my sister's fiftieth birthday, June 14. When Peggy wasn't twiddling her thumbs thinking up names, her main twiddle was over what should she do about my sister Eliza's fiftieth birthday. Her relationship with Eliza had always been a troubled one, and Peggy lived in mortal fear of doing or saying the wrong thing. So, should she give her a big party? Should she go over and stay in France? What should she give her? She was not going to win this one. A few days after she arrived back in London on May 23, in the middle of the night, she had a massive stroke and went into a coma.

What could have been the reason for the stroke? She had had a happy, but maybe tiring, trip, accompanied by jet lag. Or was it the news announcement that night, that Ghandi's son had been blown up by a woman strapped with dynamite? (She used to listen to the BBC World Service in the middle of the night, with a little transistor on her tummy.) Peggy had spent her last ten years filming in India and loved the country.

When something as cataclysmic happens for the first time, what do you do? What do we do? Molly and me? What do we do about the show? Of course, I went off to London. It felt like an unreal situation. A waking dream or nightmare: disconnected from the farm, my family, the company, and the massive effort it had taken to gather the people and resources together. Unreal too, to see my mother full of tubes, immobile and unconscious on her hospital bed. And the question of whether she should be kept alive. And if so, for how long? Or what were the chances of her recovery and in what condition?

At first, I stayed with Janet Suzman, a great friend who lived close by the hospital. Above me, where I slept or didn't sleep, was the fax machine. I would awake or open my eyes to the light and page upon page of faxes would cascade down over my head: minutes of farm meetings, questions—what do you think we should do? A, B, or C? Or D? And of course, messages of affection, concern for Peggy, and on and on and on. The doctors insisted that time be given to see if she would come out of the coma, but refused to give any specific timeframes. It was a strange situation, to witness this hovering.

One day during this time of purgatory, I visited Peggy's apartment with my dad. As we were leaving—my dad heading for the five flights of stairs—I suggested taking the lift. On the way down, I told Jeremy how I always worried that Peggy would get stuck in this very cranky, old lift.

What would she do? We arrived at the ground floor and the doors wouldn't open. We looked at each other, slightly alarmed, so I pressed the fifth-floor button and back up we went. And the doors didn't open. Getting a little panicky, I pressed the red button, and this loud old-fashioned alarm bell rang out. I looked at my dad: his hands were covering his face and ears. His head was bowed. And my flash was, This is the alarm that sounded before his ship went down. I pressed the ground floor button and down we went, and the doors still refused to open. I had no recourse. I karate kicked as hard as I could, and the doors opened. My dad was now seethingly angry and found the nearest phone where he could berate the building management. By the time he had somewhat recovered his calm, we were walking towards the hospital. He said, "Funny thing, I just realized that Peggy had her stroke on the fiftieth anniversary of the Kelly's sinking in WW II, because we're just about to hold our fiftieth annual Kelly dinner."

And here's, perhaps, where my wits began to turn. My dad's ship, HMS Kelly, had been captained by Louis Mountbatten, killed by the IRA in his own boat in the eighties. I began to get paranoid that one of the toughest old members of The Angry Brigade, who had finally been released from his prison sentence, might bomb this anniversary dinner, hosted by Prince Charles, Mountbatten's nephew. This paranoia was a sign of the gathering manic build. A week or two later, our family's exasperation was becoming unbearable. The doctors refused to let Peggy go, whereas we felt was this was the inevitable course of action. Then one day, Peggy rejected her feeding needles. She just popped them out like a thorn or a sliver and, much to our relief, the doctors agreed not to put them back in. That began the process of dehydration, which is a kind of slow dance to the end.

Witnessing someone dehydrating was extraordinary. One day, when I had been talking to the farm on the phone, Nadja Petersen, David's ten-year-old daughter, asked me what it was like for Peggy. I said, "It's like going down the Fraser Canyon. You go through these incredible, rough and turbulent, fast, foaming moments and you eventually get down to where the river broadens out and runs gently to the sea. And when you get to the sea, that's when you die." And she did. On my sister's fiftieth birthday, June 14.

Eliza and I met up at Peggy's flat. It would be hard to say who was the furthest "gone" psychologically. We were on a seesaw of keeping the other sane. We had received Peggy's letter of wishes from her solicitor. Despite it being clearly stated in the letter that Peggy's wish was to be cremated, Eliza had a complete idée fixe that she'd wanted to be buried in a spot that she and Eliza had visited, and no amount of persuasion could convince her to the contrary.

In a state of total frustration, I left the apartment and went across the landing, where a lifelong friend of Peggy's lived. She talked me down gently and I finally mentioned the Kelly and the day that it went down. "Oh, yes," she says, "I was there with Peggy and your aunt in this little house to where she had been evacuated. We were in the kitchen, your aunt Barbara her husband Victor and I. And Peggy, who was eight and a half months pregnant with your sister Eliza, was in the living room. The radio came on in the kitchen to say that the Kelly had been sunk, with all hands on board. We turned the radio down, hoping Peggy hadn't heard the news." And nothing was ever said, until a few days later when a quarter of the crew were picked up off the coast of Crete, including my dad and Mountbatten, who, soaked in oil and surrounded by intermittent machine-gun fire, had shared a raft. Supposedly, Peggy never knew about that initial announcement of the sinking of the Kelly that had come on the radio only to be turned down. Knowing Peggy's hypersensitivity, I very much doubt that this was the case.

As I said, somewhere around this time both Eliza and I were teetering on the edge of a breakdown. At a dinner at my dad and June's, Eliza became quite disturbed, and I took it upon myself to create a diversion. I faked an agonising back spasm, and was carried by Darcy, who had joined us a few weeks earlier, up to my bedroom. Eliza immediately stopped her own freakout and was totally concerned for her brother. The next thing I knew, June's psychiatrist, a very sweet old guy, was reading me the riot act: "If you don't take these medications religiously, I'll hospitalize you." I really had no choice but to take the meds. I had not touched any anti-psychotic meds for years but in the morning, I tried. It was a hefty reminder. The somewhat refined anti-psychotic was gentler than in the early seventies but it still caused a brow-twisting lobotomy. You're completely incapacitated, with your mouth dried, your tongue twisted, and your hands shaking. This would not get me through the funeral and all the other events to come. But I was under close observation. I had to take my meds publicly at the correct times. So, to convince my watchers and keep a clear head I developed the technique of "mouthing" them—putting them under the tongue, taking a sip of water, swallowing hard, then conversation, conversation, and then off to the washroom and down the toilet with them. I called it my homeopathic anti-psychotic and of course, because I was on meds, my sister became kind and attentive. It's family dynamics. Who needs the attention? That was how I saw it. And really, that's how I got through my mum's funeral.

The day before the funeral, we had a rehearsal in the church for Peggy's favourite Caravan song "Newborn Filly" (Peter Anderson's majestic workhorse anthem) from *Horseplay*. But I needed a guitar, and I had no money. So, I sent Darcy and his cousin Harriet (who had played Juliet at the Caravan two years before) to pick up some cash from Peggy's solicitor and go to Tottenham Court Road to find a guitar. Darcy came trembling back to the church with a beautiful Gibson guitar, a perfect choice. No small feat for a nineteen-year-old, unfamiliar with London. Darcy and I, along with Harriet and my other cousin, Catherine, and my nieces, Emily and Manon, Eliza's daughters, sang "Newborn Filly" at Peggy's funeral.

> *Newborn filly, trembling in the sun*
> *Listen and hear what your fathers have done*
> *How they took their place in the world of men*
> *Were beaten down but they rose up again . . .*

And then I flew back home. Of course, at the time, I was starting the "down." The inevitable down: from the euphoria-mania which had begun around the time my dad and I had been trapped in the lift, to the depths of the darkest depression. And it's fast. Coming back to the show's last rehearsals, everyone was seeking my input on this, that, and the other. There were absolutely fantastic moments in the play, which had been entirely self-directed by the company, and completely unwieldy ones. An ending had to be found, as I had mercilessly cut the entire Act III. I was going down the tubes and had not even begun to really come out of the intensity of the world I had just left behind.

When I had left six weeks before, Molly had determined to stay and keep things together on the home front, which she had managed beautifully, extraordinarily. It had been hard for her. A number of times my dad, concerned that I was in a vulnerable mental state, had wanted her to come over to England, but she had held fast. Getting back together wasn't easy. There was a gulf between us. Each of us had gone through intense experiences of very different kinds that were almost impossible to relate the one to the other.

Creation opened at the farm and then travelled to Kamloops for a two-week run on the First Nation's Reserve on the Thompson River. We pitched our tents slap bang in the middle of poison ivy, which, for those sensitive to it, creates an excruciating rash. Molly got it worst, she was covered with it. Peter Anderson took over her role as Death until she recovered.

Given the circumstances, it was a miracle that Creation fulfilled its promise. It was a tribute to all the people who worked on it collectively and harmoniously. When the organizational structure was thrown up in the air, the way that the whole company reacted was a huge, authentic experience of collective solidarity.

When it came to planning the next season I was at a loss, and advocated for a fallow year—which began a big argument with the board, who of course couldn't countenance a year with no revenues. The compromise was producing Cathy Stubbington's marionette play *In the Time of Miracles*, and a training workshop of Shakespeare's *A Winter's Tale* for directors, actors, and designers. Both would bring in revenue. And then, an exploration workshop of the third *Mystery Cycle* play, *The Passion*.

Pretty close to a year after Peggy died, my other mother, Nan, died: the wee Scots lassie who had raised me while Peggy nightly trod the boards and who had subsequently become Mum's housekeeper. She was at least ten years younger than Peggy and had always played a pivotal role in our family. Is it possible to explain the stages of loss that a person goes through when their mother dies? Possibly it's more complex when it's a man, given that men have a more difficult time coming to grips with their feeings anyway. Peggy's death was very public, Nan's was private and restrained. Some of her relatives came down from Scotland and my English family were there for the funeral. Nan and Peggy together had formed a hugely strong, affectionate, and loving place in my life, and it felt quite empty without them.

The Dam Crawford and Foal Maestro

CHAPTER 21

Pastures New

Part One: Tin Barn

I was in our house at the Caravan, writing a Canada Council grant for the new policy of long-term funding for established companies. I had to look far into the future. What did the Caravan need to do now? It came out of me almost impersonally: "We were on the road so many years, we cultivated an audience and then found the Caravan Farm, where we brought that audience and new audiences to us, and generated a new repertoire cultivated on the farm. Now is the time to revisit those works and take them back onto the road, but this time aiming at international festivals and that sort of thing. We want to raise the level of our productions and take a great big move forward." And then I read it through and went, Is that what you want to do, Nick? And Nick said, "No." I didn't want to do it. I knew I couldn't do it. I guess I have to resign.

It may be noticeable throughout these yarns how I have a tendency to make fundamental decisions precipitously, off the cuff, but I would argue that what appear as reactive resolutions are frequently the result of an accumulation of strong feelings, lurking below the conscious level. A big reason for resigning was simply burnout. I doubted my energy could measure up to the ambition of the proposed plan. Another reason was that cutbacks to arts funding were on the rise, and arts organisations were being forced to take their begging bowls to high and mighty companies who could, and did, impose their own policies. It's one thing to work with arts funding organisations for life-support and a whole other thing to beg large companies who treat the arts as a tax deductible convenience. For a number of years, we had received a grant from DuMaurier, the tobacco giant; now that they were doing their utmost to prevent children's exposure to smoking, they decided to require the Caravan to exclude our children from our shows! Our children had become an integral part of the company, something we were proud of, so was banning them worth the $40,000 grant they offered? This happened a few years after I was no longer artistic director, and mercifully I didn't have to make the decision—but the very thought made me boil with anger. The artistic director no longer had to write detailed arguments to the Canada Council, they had to spend a lot of time appealing to the capitalist elite. Somehow, after almost twenty years of struggle as a quite successful "Poor Theatre," we now had to beg the private sector for our survival.

Okay, the money issues never go away, but the burnout that had smouldered through those last few years could and had to be addressed; resigning from the school had helped to some degree, but when I was confronted by my own logic of where the Caravan should go in the next few years, there was no doubt in my mind that it was time to quit. In fact, I felt liberated.

Also, there was the question of my new farm and the need to rebalance our old motto, "Art and Potatoes" because in the last few years, potatoes had got short shrift. As well, there was still the coming season. It was an ambitious one: to complete *the Mystery Cycle* with *the Passion* at the farm and then take it to four churches in the Okanagan, and to remount Horseplay.

Meanwhile, I had moved out of our house to a little shoebox in Armstrong. Molly and I had begun a process of separation, and it was a painful one for both of us, not to mention March. If you've lived together for fifteen years in a house you've built together, with the child you've raised together, working in a theatre you share, it has to be the most painful experience of a lifetime. Like so many of our generation, there had been moments of infidelity but our fundamental attachment had endured. This time, it was I who stepped away from our domestic bliss in the throes of a passionate affair. I'd found the shoebox as a place to hang my hat. So, "every seven years a volcano." It sure

Tillage at Tin Barn

blew up in many more ways than one. If you ask for a volcano, that's what you get. On one hand it's heartbreak, and on the other it's pastures new.

I couldn't move onto the new farm yet, as I'd rented the trailer to our one-time Texan cook, Shorty. So, confined to my shoebox and with major hesitation, I agreed to attend a "Men in Transition" workshop.

There I met my future business partner, Steven Lattey, holding himself rigidly against the wall to ease his troubled back. My back was troubled too. I had to lie on the floor. I don't know to what extent the workshop wrought any changes to our transitions, but it did bring us together as good friends and eventually partners in "echinacea."

Looking beyond the last two shows of my tenure, my focus was turning to farming. I had eighty acres of beautiful farmland—a dream come true. As yet, I had no idea what direction that would take except that it would involve my horses. But spring was hastening on, and with it, rehearsals for *the Passion*. Maybe it was the liberation I was sensing from the grind of theatre and administration, but *the Passion* rehearsals took a truly liberating turn and ventured into a process that was original and inspired by the subject. Of the three plays of *the Mystery Cycle*, *the Passion* evoked resistance to the Jesus myths within all the cast. The day we were to rehearse the Last Supper, which I dreaded, my back spasmed on the way up to rehearse. We messed around with the scene getting nowhere, until, in desperation, I suggested to Lois Anderson, the actress playing Jesus that day, that she try it with a coyote mask (part of our process in rehearsal was for every actor to play every part). Lois and the coyote mask blew the scene wide open. Most of the rehearsal period after that was spent experimenting with all the company members playing all the parts, delaying, to my relief, a permanent casting before we knew in which direction to go. In the end, the few days the cast had to learn their parts was ample, made up for by knowing the play from all angles. We rehearsed the Sermon on the Mount in our local United Church. I promptly fell asleep because, like with the theatre, that is how I am conditioned to react to the atmosphere. It was sort of an audition rehearsal because there was only one person delivering the sermon. Molly killed it with her piercing directness and simplicity. I woke up.

The show opened at the farm for a few performances, but then we began our tour of different churches from different Christian denominations; we would adapt to the different spaces each time.

Somehow, miraculously, our secular Caravanesque take on Jesus found support and acceptance among the different congregations. The thoughts I'd had about the Caravan taking to the road were once more affirmed. There is a dynamic between audiences coming to a theatre and players taking their theatre to the audiences.

And lastly came the remount of *Horseplay*, with its affectionate and hilarious reflection on people and horses, which was an altogether triumphant, sold-out showstopper of a show. My sister Eliza arrived from France for a first-time visit to the Wild West. She'd had a picture of the Caravan goings-on from one of her two daughters who had already spent time at the farm. The day she arrived coincided with my moving into the double-wide trailer on "Tin Barn Farm."

Eliza Hutchinson Loizeau

Eliza was always at two minds about everything. Sometimes it put her into a frantic, anxious, and sometimes depressed state. But I think the freshness of the environment kept her spirits high, although her two minds were focussed on whether or not to leave her husband of twenty-five years. We had a great visit. Not long after, Pierre, her husband, died of a sudden onset of cancer.

By then I've officially resigned as artistic director and a small group of Caravaners was formed to direct the operations until the board could find a replacement. Well, that's one more weight off my shoulders and I could turn my full attention to the land.

I'm almost becoming my childhood dream—embodied in my favourite Jimmy Rogers' song from when I was five, "Way Out on the Mountain"—and almost fulfilling my twelve-year-old self's ambition of becoming a sheep farmer in New Zealand. For the moment, it's horses.

I have inherited from the Caravan a few Clydes and Big Jim, a Clyde stallion that I'd bought to keep the Caravan breeding program going. A good friend, another Steve, offered me a somewhat out-of-control Irish thoroughbred stallion that he had inherited but had no place to look after. And this gave me the chance to breed my Clydesdale mares to thoroughbred blood that would lead to warm-bloods used in competition.

Early in the spring, "Men-in-Transition" Steven calls me up:

"Have you heard of echinacea?"

"No. What's that?"

"Well, I got this friend out on Westside Road who's growing it. We should go out and have a look at it, because you've got some ground there, right?"

"Sure, I've got some ground."

We go out to this old hippy dope-grower's cabin on the Westside Road and sit drinking echinacea tincture, ninety proof, for about four hours. Drunk on

Catherine Watters in a drying tray of echinacea

echinacea. We thought we would plant some and see how it went. We had the
head honcho of Natural Factors, the major producer of health supplements in
BC, who told us:

"Yeah, grow echinacea, we'll pay you. How much do you want for it?"

"We want twenty-five dollars a pound for fresh flower." "Suuuure!" he says.

Beside one of the tin barns was an area that had been inhabited by the young
pigs during the time Tin Barn Farm was a pig farm. It was flat and close to water
and electricity. So, we dug it up, turned it over and planted about a quarter of
an acre of echinacea seedlings. Given the richness of the soil, we had a powerful
crop. When we started picking it, it was like picking gold. We had pounds and
pounds and pounds of fresh flowers which we sent off to Natural Factors. And
they said: "Wow! What amazing flowers you've grown. That's so great.

Thank you. Here's a big fat cheque."

And then, in the following winter, we were trying to decide how much
to plant that year. "Well, what will the price be this year?" "Oh, let's phone
Natural Factors."

I phoned up Natural Factors and tried to find out what they would buy our
echinacea for and they were surprisingly noncommittal and slightly cagey. And
Steven and I looked at each other and went:

"Yeah, we can see the writing on the wall. It won't be twenty-five bucks
a pound no more. What're we gonna do?" And at this point, "Well, in for a
penny, in for a pound. Maybe we have to seriously think about processing and
marketing our own."

Thus began Freshwoods Farm Echinacea. Peggy was right. Tin Barn Farm Echinacea would not be an easy sell. Steven was a way more hard-nosed businessman, and he basically ended up taking over the whole marketing side of things; I really only cared about the growing. By then I was no longer marking my time by shows. Now it is which part of Tin Barn have I cultivated and put into echinacea.

Since they left the farm, The Caravan Stage Company had come back to BC and then shipped out east, where they had toured Eastern Canada and the eastern seaboard as far as Florida in the States. About this time, Paul Kirby phoned me: "We're ditching the horses and wagons and we're gonna build a boat. Would you like to buy the Caravan wagons and harness?" The offer was

Nick and Molly with their teams at the ploughing match

very reasonable, so I took it. My interest was in the hitch wagon because it would allow me to compete in the Armstrong Fall Fair—a major event for our area in which we had competed in one way or another for years. It was always a big show of the horses, a time to get harness polished and cleaned, and a serious test of horsemanship. The Vardo wagon, the home on the road for the Kirby family, was to go to their eldest son Elia and his wife Lois. The shiny red Medicine wagon, with its little built-in stage, would be bought by veteran Caravaner Judy Young, who made up part of the transitional artistic direction group.

With the move to the new farm, and outside of the gathering focus on echinacea, the horses were playing an increasingly large role in my life. On top of the breeding program, there was field work— plowing, disking, harrowing, packing, seeding, and haying—all of which required different hitches of the horses from single, team, and multiple hitch configurations. I was still required with a team down at the Caravan for the yearly sleigh-ride shows. And then there was, of course, the plowing match, a yearly ritual bringing farmers together, tractors, and horses, to see who could do the best job. Molly, who'd stayed in our house at the Caravan with March following our separation, had recently bought a place (the Griz) a few miles away. She started to practice plowing with her own fine team team of Percherons. She became the first woman to beat all the boys. She sure could plow a straight furrow. Inevitably, we had to become involved in the plowing match committee, whose rituals never changed. I was drafted president for a number of years and Molly was the treasurer forever. Driving back home one day after a meeting, I wrote a song and here's the first verse:

If life has a million metaphors Plowing must surely be one
The straight and the narrow the lay of your furrow
The split before you are done
And if plowing was merely a metaphor for your life and the things that you do
From your start to your finish your land will diminish
It ain't easy to keep it all true.

By this time, Snake had arrived at the "shrunk shank" sixth age of the Seven Ages of Horse; he was in his thirties and had gone into retirement with a wonderful friend of the Caravan, Peter Claxton. Peter was a towering, gentle figure and completely blind. He had played the shepherd Corin in our production of *As You Like It* and had ridden his sweet saddle-bred mare the three miles to rehearsals or performances and home again—not that it made much difference to him whether it was day or night. He had a small herd of horses who all wore different pitched bells so he could tell who was who.

After Snake joined his bunch, he often visited the farm with his sidekick Louis, a genuine latter-day hobo, always dressed in a shabby three-piece suit from the thrift store. Peter was very tall and Louis very short, and down the driveway they would ride, blind Peter on his smallish bay mare, and deaf Louis aloft Snake, conjuring Don Quixote and Sancho Panza.

One day Peter calls me to say that Snake's condition (pneumonia) is rapidly going downhill and maybe the time has come. With a heavy heart I drive over to Peter's, where we wait apprehensively for the executioner to arrive. To our surprise he is the furthest from our expectation of a hired gun—he is almost priestlike in his gentle sympathy. Snake, who is usually so wary of vets and farriers, is surprisingly calm as we head down the hill to the chosen spot. As our friendly executioner reaches for his rifle, Snake rears up onto his hindlegs, has a violent seizure and crashes dead at my feet. He outsmarted us all!

A few days later Peter sent me a poem. These are the last three stanzas:

The Mellowing Snake; with passing years you ease a little
with grudging grace accept the ministrations of vet and farrier
And by degrees, more and more return affection with affection, trust with trust
Things not likely given nor frivolously received
Until, in years of grace, with failing teeth and failing wind, you need'st accept
the heavy choice of others to end this strange eventful history

And so, with him who chose you at your side to give the order
Have no reproach. "If t'is to be done t'were well it were done quickly"
So Go! Go swiftly to the high Pastures of Everlasting Spring
And there seek out your kind, your mares, your advisories
Pass on your spirit, but not your fears of Man, to generations to come

But when the summer winds rush in the trees, we'll hear your neighing
When the feed pails clatter, we'll hear your whinny
And when we stroke another's silken hide
we'll hear that inner rumbling which is your whicker of content.

  Farewell and au revoir Old Friend

Horses in echinacea

CHAPTER 22

Pastures New

Part Two: Freshwoods Farm

Farming, tough and taxing as it was, suited me well. The burnout that I'd experienced with the accumulation of running the Caravan, the National Theatre School, combined with the deaths of Nan and Peggy and culminating in my separation from Molly, had dissipated. The outdoors and the practical work felt good, and the horses were always rewarding. The farming life was restoring body and mind. The echinacea business started to take off over the next few years. We had found a processor on the coast who turned our flowers into tincture.

We evolved a logo which featured two of our horses, shoulder deep in echinacea flower, and Steven was hustling all over BC and getting our bottles on the shelves. But of course, Natural Factors was squeezing our presence off the shelves, inch by inch.

One of the major expenditures of any farming operation that's growing new crops is labour. I had some amazing teams of weeders, mainly drawn from my daughter March's friends and Caravaners needing more pocket money. But as the land under cultivation grew exponentially year by year, so did the costs. So, there was a constant quest to find appropriate equipment either horse-or tractor-drawn.

Getting my hands in the dirt and my mind on fundamental questions, such as cultivation, had restored my energy and lifted my spirits. Of course, there were hangover strands from the old life, but broadly speaking Nick had found farming and loved it.

We were also diversifying our crop: other medicinal herbs astragalus, catnip, and garlic. Steven had encountered a distributor of cat toys who bought the entire crop of catnip for a number of years.

Our big capital expense was building a dryer that could accommodate all the different crops that could only be sold in dried form.

One day, a guy who was making power bars approached us to see if we would dry the organic vegetables that he was buying in bulk from California. By this point we were beginning to suffer, as all growing operations do, from the fact that growth was in fact reducing our margins, given the need for new equipment and mounting labour and marketing costs. We were ready for anything that would inject new revenue and maintain our crew. The process involved about a ton of vegetables of various kinds that would need to be pristinely washed, sorted, packed into the fifty-odd drying trays, and closely monitored.

Then the contractor required that they be powdered and finally shipped. I had found an old grain grinder on the farm that pulverized the load fairly well. It was primitive though, and we did receive some complaints that occasional pieces of screen material were found in the powders. I figured it was time for some expert consultation. The consultant arrived, took a walk around the operation, turned to me and said, "Do you want to dry vegetables for your career?" Well, immediately my heart sank. Of course, I didn't want to dry vegetables for the rest of my life. But anyway, he gave us a detailed description of what we needed—all of which would involve a small fortune's worth of stainless steel.

That day, a ton of carrots from California had gone into the dryer and that evening I forgot to open the vents, which is essential with carrots because of the amount of moisture they release. The carrots were ruined and that was a big loss. And it just confirmed that without a shadow of a doubt, I was not fit to make a life out of drying vegetables.

The farm consisted of eighty acres. About ten of them were in intensive cultivation for herbs and garlic. The remainder was in hay and grain, and we sought a grain crop that could be planted in the fall and might have a niche value. We hit on spelt, an ancient wheat barely known about at the time,

Freshwoods Farm in full production

containing considerably less gluten than the others. There were about half a dozen organic farmers in our neck of the woods who were exploring the crop. But conventional grain cleaners couldn't clean the husks. After exhaustive research, we found a German company that had developed the technology. Thus was born the Organic Spelt Co-op. The machinery was set up on a neighbouring farm to which we brought the spelt and from which it was distributed. Everything worked quite well at the outset, but of course as the market developed we became less able to compete with the demand. Things were getting tight, but salvation was at hand.

Two local ginseng growers approached us. Previous to the echinacea fad, there had been a massive wave of ginseng production. All sorts of farmers and non-farmers had invested in acres of the shade-cloth and poles that were required to grow ginseng. And then it all collapsed. The two growers who came to us were intent on developing a medicinal herb business. They offered to buy Freshwoods Farm. Not the land, of course, but the label. Steven would become their marketing director, and they committed to buying all the herb from Freshwoods Farm.

Business negotiations are never easy, and after much angst and tribulation the deal was signed. Phew! But of course, reality stepped in and the new company hit obstacles, wouldn't buy the herb crop that they committed to, and over time everything fell apart. One day, at our plowing match meeting, Mike arrived. He and his wife ran a major vegetable operation that supplied local supermarkets with great produce. He was determined to convert the backbone of their operation from tractor power to horse power. We became friends and traded some of my horse equipment for tractor equipment that I needed, as I was beginning to move in the opposite direction.

Sometime later, he and his wife arrived at my farm with a beautiful notebook with "Nick's Summer" on the front page. It was a very detailed plan for a season of vegetable production. Mike and his wife were debating whether to transition from conventional growing to organic. They were proposing that I, as a certified organic grower, be the guinea pig, to determine if there was a sufficient local organic market. They would therefore help me through the season—when to grow, harvest, etc.—and then they would distribute the crop. Given the circumstances, it was a great proposal; all worked smoothly, and I happily learned a prodigious amount in the process. Trouble was, there wasn't a sufficient demand for organic vegetables in the North Okanagan, so I had no choice but to sell my thousands of beautiful cauliflowers to Vancouver, where the demand for organic veggies was going through the roof. But the cost of shipping those beautiful cauliflowers ate up all the profit. You can't win.

Of all the crops that we grew, taking all expenses into consideration, the most profitable was garlic. Molly, back in the day, had developed a very resilient

Garlic Harvest

prize-winning garlic which became the foundation of our crop. March and her friends proved to be the ultimate garlic braiders, so hanging in our barn come harvest time would be a beautiful mass of garlic braids. One day, a very nice couple from the coast who ran a health food store dropped by the farm and offered to take our entire production. The braids sold like hot cakes, and March and her friends developed a six-foot braid of garlic. Garlic was rolling. Then one year at harvest time when we took the garlic out of the ground and hung it in the barn, little by little, each bulb developed a blue hue and, in a month or two, the bulbs were done for. It was a disease transmitted from farm to farm. No one at the time could put their finger on the cause but the lesson was: don't get too big too quick, regenerate your seed more frequently, and nourish your soil better and always rotate your crops! There is a well-known farmer's joke that goes along with farming and its costs:

"What would you do if you won the lottery?" Answer: "Keep farming till it's all gone."

But the garlic debacle was seriously demoralizing. On top of which, I was discovering that each year, there was less and less pasture grass available for the horses. My hill-top farm was drying out and instead of beginning to feed hay in October, I was needing to feed it in July. Besides, there was the creeping feeling I had already encountered of sheer exhaustion and the need for real pastures new.

So began a search for them. Part of me was craving the sea, but anywhere close was way out of my price range and few places could accommodate my twenty-odd horses. On my quest, I visited my good friends and old Caravaners, Zev and Sharon. They lived in the mountains quite far north from my place, near a tiny village that consisted of a primary school and a store, but which had a special character. This was Dunster, BC.

Zev shoed horses and raised them, and Sharon wrote plays and taught theatre in the local schools. Near the end of my stay, they suggested I look at a property that was coming up on the market not too far from where they lived. It was a breathtaking hundred and sixty acres running along the most famous river in BC, the Fraser. There wasn't much there apart from the land, with a gorgeous creek that ran down to the river, an ugly twelve-by-forty-eight-foot trailer, and a little cabin. But it took my breath away, and I could see the horses getting a new lease on life with the abundant feed there. Though the land thrilled me, the thought of all the mechanics of buying and selling and moving to an extraordinarily beautiful place, compared to where I'd been for so long, gave me pause. But returning to Tin Barn, I realised that all the rational reasons I'd thought of for the move paled in comparison to the deep need I felt for a fundamental change. It was coming close on thirty years I'd been at the Caravan and Tin Barn, and sixty was hovering into sight. The sense of adventure which had been a driver in my life had all but disappeared, but the wild mountains and sweeping river and the good friends that lay two hundred miles north offered plenty of challenge and adventure.

The only way to buy the land was to sell Tin Barn, which wasn't an easy matter—and I needed to sell it by the time the deal on the land near Dunster came due. The seller of the Dunster land was pushing hard for her money. In the nick of time I found a buyer, and following the thrills and spills of real-estate machinations, the deal squeaked through.

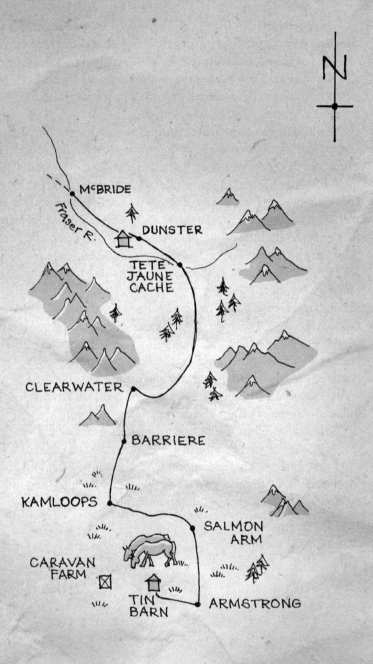

Tin Barn to Dunster

CHAPTER 23

Dunster

I had been joined over the last few years at Tin Barn by a resident farmhand of sixty-five years or more, Slim, who lived in his old bus with his dog, a chained-up blue healer, Blue. Slim had a wealth of practical abilities, and could spin a believable yarn all the way till it ran out. He could disappear for days on a beer binge and when there was a party at the Caravan Farm along our border, he was known to let off both barrels of his shotgun to quiet the noise from next door. When he heard the news of the possible move to Dunster, he was over the moon. It would take him back to the wilderness he loved. So, I figured I had to be on the right track because without some help I had no idea how to move all that I had to move—all my essential farm machinery, the horses and all their tack and equipment, and all my personal stuff. By the time it was organised and loaded, I had to make quite a number of trips, and leaving Tin Barn, I barely registered any regret. The focus was the future.

I had my ancient Ford 250 pick-up truck and the trailer, with which I must've completed seven or eight five-hundred-click return trips, and then I hired a huge low-bed, eighteen-wheel transport truck for the heavy farm equipment. I was sitting in my decrepit mobile home up in Dunster, waiting for that truck to arrive with Slim aboard. What was striking about this new place I'd landed? The silence, more profound than anywhere I'd ever been, and the monumental mountains. The eighteen-wheeler and Slim finally arrived a day late. My long driveway dropped down a fairly steep hill and took a right turn at the bottom. That's where the transport got stuck. We worked into the dark trying, with my relatively puny tractor, to help it gain a foothold and mercifully by morning it was in the yard. Then began the equally laborious move to bring out twenty horses to their promised land.

Because of the number of trips that were needed complete the move, I barely noticed that I had left my farm, the Caravan, and my life of almost thirty years. If I had thought about it, I would have said, "No regrets. It was altogether amazing, but now it's onto the next."

A few years before this, Northern BC had been struck by an infestation of what is known as the pine beetle. In normal weather conditions, only a few pine beetles survive the hard frosts of December and January, but if those don't occur, the beetles proliferate and start killing the pines. Massive swaths of forest had been killed when I arrived. And many trees on the land were standing dead. So, the first order of business was to sell as many truckloads as I could to the local mill. But there was a limit to what they would take as they were inundated with pine kill from all directions. So, given that I needed to build some proper infrastructure, I managed to buy a wood mill, and that became a major project for Slim. And in so doing we were able to build a large hayshed and equipment shed.

Winter in Dunster

Here's a classic Slim story. One Christmas at the new place in Dunster, when Sue and Al and my son Darcy were visiting, we were sitting in my little cabin attached to my ugly long trailer, playing our tunes. Slim came in with a sheet of paper, and he says, "I've written a song. And I want that girl with the banjo [Sue]. She can do the tune. I sure like that girl on the banjo, because I like the banjo." So, we took his words and spent the evening setting them to to a good ol' country waltz tune. The chorus was "My rifle, my pony and me"—a classic cowboy waltz. Anyway, we sang it to the full and got it perfected. Slim was over the moon and went back to his bus with a recording we made and played it all night long and into the next day. It was definitely the great Slim hit. Many moons later, I came across an old Western classic called "My Rifle, My Pony and Me." It was someone else's song.

It was a bit tragic what happened to him. Slim, of course, was an erstwhile alcoholic or binge-alcoholic. And there were periods of time when Slim would not come out of his bus for love or money. I would say to myself, Oh, Slim's having a depression—or bad back or whatever it was. But sometimes it involved cases of beer. One night sitting in my dirty old trailer, I hear engines coming down the hill, blinding headlights and then a loud knock on the door. I open the door and there is Pete the Heat, the very same police sergeant on whom I had planted a packet of green stuff during the sleigh-ride hold-up at Caravan. So, there is Pete the Heat plus an ambulance, because Slim has called 911 as he is in such agony that he needs to go into the hospital. Oh my God, poor Slim. Off to the hospital he goes. A few weeks later, I get a phone call from the hospital saying, "We've just run all these tests on Slim and there's absolutely nothing wrong with his back and he's to go home tomorrow." I know that unless Slim goes into treatment and deals with the alcohol, I can't have him coming back. I can't do it. So off to the hospital to confront Slim. And by way of a starter, I say, "You're in such a pickle here. If anything happens to you, I need to know your kids' phone numbers and addresses." I know he has a couple of kids. "I need to be able to get in touch with somebody. I won't be your parent anymore." And the man with the bad back comes flying out of the bed, and I think, Oh, I'm going up against the wall. But he flies by me and grabs his pants that are hanging on the wall and pulls out his wallet. "Here!" It is his son's address. It is all very dramatic and, in the end, Slim goes off to live with a fairly heavy drinker in the area. I call his son who says to me: "Oh, I'm so glad to talk to you. You know, you shouldn't worry about what happened with Slim. You've lasted longer than anyone else."

One thing that was as unexpected as it was joyful was that my great friend Sherry Bie was appointed as new artistic director at the National Theatre School. In my day she had taught storytelling there, and it was thrilling that she was ready to do that tough job. She asked me to work with the second year actors on a Shakespeare play, which of course is what I like doing most. I also went round the country with her, auditioning prospective students. Over seven years, from 2001 to 2008, I did *Henry VI, Part 1 and 2, Antony and Cleopatra, King Lear, Twelfth Night, All's Well That Ends Well,* and *Macbeth.* What a break that gave me, and a reconnection with teaching and directing that had been absent for a long time. Getting back to Montreal was exciting as long as it didn't last too long.

A less happy dynamic was finding myself in the midst of an addiction drama that involved two of my sons. Here the story goes back to Tin Barn days . . .

Darcy, twenty-one, a talented musician and a practical genius, had worked for a number of years in the outdoor marijuana business, which employed a generation of young adults in all aspects of production. They made great money, had an amazing community, and could afford, in the off season, to travel the world. But of course, the dream didn't last forever. With the arrival of cocaine as a vastly more valuable commodity, it began to be traded for marijuana and inevitably consumed by the crews, including Darcy.

On the other side of the Atlantic, Stéphane, twenty-seven, was working in the French movie business, where he too fell victim to the curse of coke. In a major contretemps with his mother Sylvianne, with desperation he asked her, "If there's anything you haven't told me, tell me now." At which point Sylvianne reveals to Stephane that this theatre director in Canada, called Nick, is in fact his biological father. He manages to get my coordinates and writes me about his discovery and his desire to come and visit.

Stéphane's arrival at the farm (Tin Barn) was a truly joyful encounter. There was clearly no doubt about his paternity. He looked like a combination of me and my father, and he could relate with no difficulty to the farm work and spirit of the place. In the course of the visit, he met up with his brother Darcy and they enjoyed many adventures together, the last being a trip to Calgary where Darcy was intending to start a course in film. On his return, Stephane was in a serious state of anxiety because he realized that his brother Darcy was in a major cocaine crisis.

Without going into detail, there began a journey by the end of which one reaches the agonizing realization that any effort to save, prevent, or sustain someone in the throes of addiction is fruitless. Trying to look out for Darcy, plunged me into the seamy side of the Vancouver drug scene, and the stress and emotional upheaval eventually landed me in the psychiatric ward of the Lion's Gate Hospital in North Vancouver. A reminder that intense emotional stress is a principal driver of manic depression. Following Darcy's quest for help with his addiction, I ended up flying to Cape Town, South Africa, to be part of a treatment program to assist as a family member.

Switching strands to Peggy. The last event I mentioned was her funeral, but the reverberations continued. A year or so after that, a massive memorial celebration of her life was held in Westminster Abbey with supremely moving contributions from John Gielgud, Peter Hall, Julian Bream, Judi Dench, and on and on. It was a bit over the top with the full ecclesiastical pageantry, the power of the place and the throngs of people inside and out, but nevertheless it was something to know how much she meant to so many people. When I came back from South Africa, the final piece of her departure was the laying of a stone in her memory in Poets' Corner, a beautiful spot in Westminster Abbey where writers and artists are remembered.

Arriving at the abbey, I was steered to the Henry IV room where I found one of Peggy's dearest friends and collaborators, guitarist extraordinaire Julian Bream. During the war, Peggy and Natasha Spender had founded the Apollo Society, which gave performances of poetry and music. Julian had been Peggy's collaborator on many occasions. Back at the abbey, hunched over his guitar, fingers flying up and down his fingerboard, he said in his inimitable voice with its traces of cockney, "Nick, I gotta keep doin this for a bit longer cause otherwise I won't make it with the Bach."

I was to read a Shakespeare sonnet, and had a great deal of trouble finding the one most apt. The Sonnet that I chose begins thus:

If music and sweet poetry agree
As they needs must, the sister and the brother
Then must the love be great twixt thee and me
For thou dost love the one and I the other.

Another switch of strand . . . my father's wife June and her protracted illness. June and Jeremy were as close as a couple could ever be. She suffered severe depressions, during which time my father became a patient caregiver, maybe for the first time in his life. But with the beginnings of June's dementia, a fall, and the onset of mini strokes, I found myself in England on more frequent occasions. On one such, with June hospitalized, Jeremy, who adored opera, grabbed three days away from the bedside to go to the Glyndebourne Festival in Sussex.

Normally, he would drive back to London in the morning but chose to leave later than usual and fell asleep at the wheel, careening off the road. He was extracted from the car by "the jaws of life" and returned to June's bedside with a small cut on his forehead. He was in his early nineties. He was charged with careless driving and discharged on condition that he undertook a new driving test. Thenceforth, he was only allowed by the family to drive locally in Sussex. Not long after, June died, and I began a whole new relationship with Jeremy.

Although grief-stricken, he opened up emotionally to me. It can take a long time for fathers and sons to break the ice.

Returning to home base—Dunster. The joy and peace of living in a wilderness of mountains and rivers is one thing, the isolation and deafening silence is quite another. One day, while putting a young horse through its paces, teamed up with a more experienced one, I took off for a short training session; it was so uneventful that I decided to push on further. My nearest neighbour lived about two miles away; as I passed his place I noticed there was some activity in the yard and resolved to call in on my way home. I found him lying under his tractor with a broken hip, having slipped while getting down. I called the ambulance, and he was taken off to our local hospital. The next day I was trimming the feet of my dear Clyde, Big Jim, and he jerked his leg and landed me underneath him. Fortunately, there were a couple of friends who were there, and I was none the worse for wear. But the combination of those two incidents made me think hard about what an aging single man was doing playing with horses and machinery far from civilization. Recognising that age was becoming an ever-present factor in life was hard to admit, and there were more and more frequent bouts of depression—which at their worst were paralysing and demoralising, and at their best made me feel like I was wading through sludge.

Sitting in my dingy, dank trailer, my task was to decide which Shakespeare would be a feasible option for the next spring exercise at NTS. And I started to think about the Scottish play for which, of course, everyone who touches it needs to be wearing extra special kid gloves. Does it really contain magic energies? How much does it covertly or overtly deal with mental illness? Nothing was too clear, but given the turbulence of my experiences, I was powerfully drawn to the play.

Without realizing it, a new kind of frequency in my manic-depressive seesaw was starting. Since my last hospitalisation in Vancouver there had barely been a manic moment, but periods of black depression made life barely tolerable. I could attribute my depressions to the isolation factor and the grim and ugly conditions of my dingy, dank trailer. But it was not the whole picture. One of Macbeth's speeches kept reverberating. He is addressing the doctor who is caring for Lady Macbeth and her sleepwalking:

Macbeth:
Canst thou not Minister to a Mind diseased,
Plucke from the Memory a rooted Sorrow,
Raze out the written troubles of the Brain
And with some sweet Oblivious Antidote
Cleanse the stufft bosome, of that perilous stuffe
Which weighes upon the heart?

Doctor:
Therein the Patient must minister to himselfe

There was my answer! It was comforting to discover this little-known, brilliant passage where Shakespeare nails the essential elements of mental disease. It brought me the realisation that with Twelfth Night (a comedy of madness), Hamlet, King Lear, and Macbeth, the Grand Master of Theatre plumbs the depths of madness perhaps more than any writer has ever done.

Spring arrives and Macbeth it is. With the play to get my teeth into, I'm starting to wind up. Everything begins to look like it's related to everything else and is significant. This almost LSD-like perception is a well-known symptom approaching the manic high; unfortunately, the manic depressive is all too relieved to no longer suffer the slings and arrows of depression, and so enjoys the heightened perception. It never occurs to them that it is likely to leave a trail of destruction as they lose the plot and become manic.

One of March's early paintings from Concordia

CHAPTER 24

Manic Montreal

D aughter March was now in Montreal as a student at Concordia University, and I was staying with her. Her apartment was on a street which runs past this monolithic red-brick Polish Catholic Church, where I saw a mass of people carrying branches as though to Macbeth's Dunsinane. I was fascinated, so I followed them into the church—to find they were celebrating Palm Sunday. This set me on a quest to see how the myths of Easter were reflected in a play that doesn't appear to have anything at all to do with religion. It wasn't obvious, because of course religion was a forbidden subject in Elizabethan and Jacobean society where Catholics were hung, drawn and quartered if discovered. So when Shakespeare needed to confront religious issues he had to employ that fundamental theatre tool, disguise. At the same time, he was writing a play to celebrate the lineage of the new king, James, who at the time was fascinated by witchcraft—a subject that, unlike its opposite, religion, was free for discussion in public. Witchcraft is at the core of Macbeth. But alongside the ambiguity of the witches, the images of Easter and rebirth are evident in the trees of Dunsinane marching to liberate the country and in the third apparition, where the witches show Macbeth a child with a crown holding the branch of a tree.

With a mind full of transformative visions, I found a beautiful condo in the area and to my astonishment, when I approached the mortgage broker, I was not dismissed off hand. It was of course in the period of the cheap mortgage and just before the mighty crash. March and Sherry both tried their utmost to dissuade me from such an extravagant and ultimately unaffordable venture. But for me, the desire to live in a beautiful house in a vibrant community as opposed to my dingy-dank-trailer in the middle of nowhere was overwhelming.

I go back to Dunster with this deal pending. I'm starting to freak out because I see the realities when I get my feet back on the ground.

I'm starting to have serious doubts. Can I pull out of this deal? I have to go back to Montreal to conclude the deal, and I'm in as big a tizzy as I've ever been in over whether to pursue the purchase or to ignominiously back out. Why is backing out of a deal so hard? People do it all the time. But for some reason I am paralyzed. I pluck up my courage, meet the real estate guy and tell him I can't do it. Which of course is nothing. But to me it feels like the end of the world. He's quite good about it: "Just don't worry. Don't worry." And as I drive home from Edmonton airport, he's phoning me up, saying, "Are you sure? Have you really thought about it?" And he somehow reopens the door a crack. When I get back, I'm beginning to think, Well maybe I should do it. I mean, my clothes are already there, I'm already half moved in, and the daughter of a good friend has been lined up to rent a room in the house. So, I swing the other way and buy it.

Chico on route across Canada

One of the best things that ever happened to me up in Dunster was finding Chico, a three-year-old white and orange Australian shepherd/border collie cross. He became my eyes and ears, my psychiatrist, and altogether much-beloved pal. His feline companion, Actali, had been with me since Tin Barn days and eventually tolerated Chico.

They had to come to Montreal too, in a transcontinental move with the furniture and all the sundries a person needs when moving into an empty space. I realized I was going to have to move horses here, there, and everywhere, and found a deal for a twenty-four-foot stock trailer which would serve to make the haul. For the time being, Zev agreed to check on and feed the horses; since I was feeding them round hay bales, it would only require minimal attention.

I needed company for the trip and an ex-military, ex drug/alcohol warrior who I'd met in Montreal agreed to join us. The furniture was piled in the trailer, Chico and Actali stashed in the back of the truck, and off we drove across Canada in the fall of 2007. The only time I'd made this trip before had been on my thumb with Sandy in the spring of 1971, and that had been in the other direction. This time it was fall, full on fall colours, breathtakingly beautiful, and when you got to Ontario, achingly long. It was hard, when necessary, to keep my windows closed as Actali had learned to operate the window switches, which relieved his boredom no end. Otherwise, the journey was uneventful except that as we drew nearer and nearer to Montreal, I grew increasingly anxious about operating this long rig of over thirty-five feet within city confines, and most alarmingly, how will I get the trailer into the Montreal back alley, behind my new place? But with a scrape and a squeeze and an irate lady who waited with protestations, we slid in.

Jeanne Mance/St Viateur is the best place to live in Montreal.

March was squeezing espresso in the local Italian coffee bar when she wasn't painting at university. There were lots of musicians playing in various hangouts, and many theatre artists from my Montreal days lived close by. I discovered that my newly built condo was constructed on the site of a Hassidic gymnasium and Hassidic families lived to my left and to my right. In fact, the area had originally been a central spot for the Hassidic Jewish community. Chico, fresh from the wide-open spaces, needed a great deal of exercise and, of course, serious training in terms of traffic and the big city. Most Hassidic Jews have both an extreme distaste and deep fear of dogs. Being the sensitive soul that he was, he eventually realized that, on encountering a Hassidic Jew, he should pull off the sidewalk and sit down, looking the other way. Sweet, eh?

A couple of years before all this happened, while I was still in Dunster, my friend and current boss, Sherry, said to me, "You should write a play about Peggy and Jeremy." Well, the seed went in, though I had difficulty with the thought of writing (this was not my preferred outlet) and of course confronting the stories of my parents.

I hadn't made any headway on her idea until I got the phone call from my old friend Dinah, asking me to contribute my thoughts on Stanislavsky for her design project in Moscow. The seed set by Sherry started to germinate, and I managed to get a Canada Council grant to write *A Mingled Yarn*. One major element in making the move to the new space in Montreal was having a clean, attractive place to write and the proximity to resources for research.

I struggled with *A Mingled Yarn* as a play. There was one scene, probably the opening, which involved my mother in a wig and gown taken from the costume trunk, delivering "The quality of mercy is not strained . . ." (Portia, *The Merchant of Venice*). I can't remember whether Jeremy was in his barrister's wig and gown, but that was as far as it got. Over time, the play evolved to a four-character combo with mother, father, son, and daughter dynamics, which immediately breathed a bit of life into it. It further developed with a cast including the Komisarjevskys, Michel St. Denis, and Peter Brook, since I was becoming fascinated by the evolution of theatre in the twentieth century through the works of the greats. But when I outlined the project to Helena Kaut-Howson, a Polish director in England who I had invited a couple of times to the school, she looked me squarely in the eyes and said, "No, Nick. It's a book."

I heard but resisted the suggestion and delved into a concept of an exhibit with actors. But in the end, I succumbed to Helena's emphatic suggestion. Without fully realizing it, I was starting to swing from one end of the spectrum to the other. Bouts of depression, out of which I struggled, would switch into high energy, sometimes creative and sometimes destructive.

Although I was only employed at the school for another spring Shakespeare, I had a workspace there, but little by little there grew a tension in my dealings with Sherry. Things came to a head the following spring when I decided to do Hamlet with the students and my grandson Chay, Darcy's son, was born. After seeing a photograph of him I resolved that I must see him. So, I booked a flight back to BC. Leaving my place in the hands of March and one of her friends, hurriedly packing my bags because the flight was early, not sleeping the night, I ran into trouble with airport security. At that time, you were only allowed one carry-on bag, so after much discussion, I managed to attach my computer bag to my carry-on, stripping off my belt to keep the whole thing together. Security let me through, but as I was retrieving my stuff, an official from WestJet took me, to all intents and purposes, into custody. I was not going to be allowed to board my flight, and I had to wait a few hours for another. It turned out that that morning a government official from the AEA was monitoring security, and I had been pegged as suspicious. The plane I was eventually put on, heading for Calgary, stopped over in Winnipeg. I was delighted because I knew that in Winnipeg it was easy to have a smoke break, of which I was quite in need. Shortly before landing, it was announced that we would not be deplaning in Winnipeg and passengers were asked to be patient, stay onboard, and allow new passengers to get on.

By this time, I was losing my patience. The hypomanic condition I was in, wasn't registering. It never does. I stood up and announced that I would be leaving the plane anyway, strode down the cabin, with attendants gently attempting to prevent me. I found myself in the airport lobby, wondering what to do next. I saw a "special lounge" sign that caught my eye, and I went in. A very accommodating young girl provided me with coffee and croissants. I went into the bathroom to splash my face, gather my thoughts, and empty my pockets to see what I had with me. I was getting the unmistakeable feeling that

I'd worked my way to the end of a branch and might fall off at any moment. It had already been a very long day and night. But when I re-emerged, there were four beefy cops laden with all their tools of the trade advancing towards me. I entrusted myself to comedy: "Please, don't taser me."

And I did make them laugh. Phew! "We won't taser you, but you have to leave the airport." Of course, I'd left coat, hat, and sundry other things onboard the plane, but as they escorted me towards the escalator, I managed to dispatch one of them to find my stuff. He was unsuccessful. They left me standing outside the airport in freezing Winnipeg weather without a coat, wondering what to do. By hook and by crook and a lot of rental car driving, I saw Chay and brought his Mum, Harmonia, some flowers.

Being as mad as I had been from the start of this odyssey one might well ask, "What did it feel like? Did you know you were crazy? Did you care if you were? Did you want to stop? Were your actions a result of paranoia?" And I would have to reply, "All of the above and much more!"

On my way back to Montreal, my dilapidated mind remembered that I had invited my third son, Carl, to come and stay. Carl and I had only met on a few occasions, first when he was a babe in arms and then more recently when March and I had gone to visit him and his mum and sister in Vermont. He had been raised in California where he'd been a schoolteacher until his passion for surfing got the better of him, and he was in search of somewhere to settle— which eventually turned out to be Nicaragua.

The visit to Montreal, on both our counts, was intended for us to get to know each other properly. How could I have forgotten the visit? Fortunately, because our life is of a mingled yarn, daughter March heroically had my back and not only that, she spent Carl's visit forging what would be for her, her closest sibling relationship. Throughout this odyssey, word travelled amongst my friends and family that "Nick's off the deep end." Attempted interventions occurred along the way but it caused much wear, tear and worry to all concerened from which I've managed to escape.

Arriving back in Montreal at the café where March was once a barista, there's a sombre welcoming committee that once more I manage to evade, with a surreptitious exit out the back. But the writing is on the wall. Sherry has put to me the question, "Nick, are you able to direct Hamlet?" And of course, though I have somewhat recovered my senses, I am still extremely fragile. I have to say no. The older you get the longer it takes to heal a cut and the same applies to healing a damaged mind; Hamlet wouldn't exactly help in those circumstances.

No, my time was up.

It's 2008, it's pack up the house, put it on the market (not a very good market), and set my sights on a return to Dunster. One day, I was walking along by the coffee bar, and Chico met these two lovely kids who really knew how to treat a dog. They were special. I struck up a conversation with their French mum, a homeless adventuress, and the next thing I knew, they were going to join me on the trip back to Dunster. In the interim, they stayed at my place, during which time they were joined by their grandmother, fresh from Morocco. They were all penniless, but great company. The mother also had a guy in her life, hopelessly in love with her, who volunteered to help with the moving and the driving. I was now re-crossing Canada in the early spring with a French quasi-commune of two kids, four adults, a dog, and a cat. They were journeying with hope and anticipation of a new life. Their enthusiasm and energy were a great comfort, and it continued once we were back in Dunster. I, on the other hand, collapsed into bed for two weeks of severe depression. I was at a loss to know what to do and where to be. The Montreal mortgage was steep, the financial crisis was reaching a peak. Under the circumstances, I doubted that I could sell the Dunster property. Eventually the French family moved on, and I sat on my deck with Chico who looked quizzically and sympathetically at my distress, willing me to action.

Then a small convoy of mafia-like, black-window-shaded SUVs came barrelling down the driveway and drove past, leaving me wondering who could possibly have such barefaced audacity and why. They returned, and a check-shirted local fixer got out of the lead vehicle, informing me that the gentlemen behind the shaded glass might be interested in buying the land. They turned out to be a small group of mega-millionaires, one from the Guggenheim Foundation and most of the others from Texas oil fields. In fact, I discovered they were buying up all the surrounding farms, ostensibly for the purpose of having a place to hunt once or twice a year. The conspiracy theorist within me suspected a longer-term interest in the water that flowed down the Fraser River and the idea of a Rocky Mountain trench that could bring fresh water to the increasingly dry lands of California and Nevada. But, boy, from the conviction that this land was unsellable to getting a fairly decent offer was a sign of changing fortune. And on the heels of the offer came the news from Montreal that my condo had sold.

So, what do I do now? Pack up the farm? What do I do with my horses? I still don't know what direction I'm going. Since Macbeth and the ensuing months of manic depression, I feel I've disqualified myself from theatre, and at the same time I've run my course in farming exploits. But before I sign the final sales contract, I need to know where to go. The only thing that makes sense, and might have been obvious to any sane person, is to leave isolation behind and connect with my growing family—two grandsons, my son, my daughter—and all the Caravan tribe in the Okanagan and Shuswap. Synchronistically, Molly was selling the house and land she had moved to when we separated sixteen years before. We were still close friends and thought that if we put the proceeds of our sales together, we might find something big enough and attractive enough to balance the risk. And find one we did.

The house was on five acres near Enderby BC, most of which were treed, so only space for a small number of horses. With great anguish, I had to face the fact that my beloved herd had to be sold. Zev, bless his heart, agreed to take them to auction in Alberta, something I would have been incapable of doing. I kept four. So once again pack, liquidate, and move.

Home in Enderby

CHAPTER 25

Enderby

The place where we landed had a good garden patch and a great view of the Enderby cliffs. We settled in. Plenty for each of us to be occupied with. But my bipolar swings had been intensifying, making it hard for anybody to live with me, as well as the inevitable red button issues between two people who'd lived together for fifteen years, which started to catch up with us.

My estimation that the land could handle four horses was wrong, and I had to whittle down to two. One of which, Fred Eaglesmith, the last foal I had bred, was in training. One beautiful summer morning, I took him out for a long walk, the exercise being, to stop at intervals and get on and off. He behaved perfectly, so when I got back to the barn, I said to myself, "Come on, let's see if you can just take a step or two under saddle." I got on and gave him the cue to move, and then I was in a bucking rodeo, round and round the corral at full tilt, until finally off I flew, landing smack on my back. I couldn't breathe. I couldn't move.

Fred ambled over to my inert body and very gently tugged with his teeth on my shirt exactly at the point which turned out to be a burst vertebra. One property over from our fence, carpenters were hammering away; finally I managed a strangled cry in between hammer strikes and they came to my rescue. It was a solid blow to remind me that I was on the edge of grandiosity and attempting the impossible.

Soon after, I spent time with my dad in London and Sussex. Sitting around the table having lunch with him and June's son Christopher, my stepbrother, we discussed all the offshoots of our family. Christopher and his partner Manel had recently become fathers to a son, and we were going over my checkered paternity. My ninety-five-year-old dad was gallantly trying to work it all out, so I proposed a grand family reunion which would allow all the different offspring and mothers to meet each other and to meet Jeremy. To my great surprise, he was enthusiastic. Big parties were not usually his thing. So, when the subject turned to practicalities and how such an event could be paid for, he proposed selling a picture. Jeremy was an avid lover of art, and he'd inherited a quite extraordinary collection of Post-Impressionist paintings from his father. We had two exceptional drawings by Matisse: one was a superb portrait of my grandmother Mary (see page 9) that my grandfather had commissioned back in the early thirties for two hundred pounds, the other, perhaps less significant, was Nude with Dog. This was to be the sacrificial lamb. It was duly put up for sale at Sotheby's. Three months later I finally managed to visit my son Carl for the first time—Carl, who had forsaken his school teaching career in San Francisco for his passion for surfing and was building a surf business in Nicaragua. It was a special few weeks getting to know each other after the debacle of Montreal. Sitting in the sandy, sweet heat with my funky little laptop, to my great surprise I managed to connect to the Sotheby's sale just in time to witness the auction of Nude with Dog, the bidding rising to unimaginable heights.

Our good friend Mandy, an old time Caravaner who now ran a summer theatre on Salt Spring Island, had persuaded Molly and me to do a production in the summer, soon after the end of the proposed grand family reunion. We settled on The Caucasian Chalk Circle. On top of which, Jeremy who made a yearly practice of taking his grandchildren to his most favourite spot in the world, Venice, decided that it was Molly's and my turn.

Previous to our departure, I'd gone to Salt Spring to do some workshops and drum up enthusiasm for the coming production. It was hypomania time unleashed, full of amazing visions—as in the idea of starting the show with a flotilla of sailing boats bringing the cast to shore at the park where we were going to perform. It was a splendid vision, but when I excitedly presented the idea to the production manager, it was obvious that not only was it completely impractical, it also made him a bit concerned for my mental health. He was right. The bipolar ups and downs were getting closer together, with hardly any time of normality in between. By the time we met up with Jeremy on the train to Venice, I was on the way down again. Molly's love for art was a perfect match for Jeremy's. I trailed along, doing my best to be enthusiastic. There was something incredibly moving in the way Jeremy took us to see his favourite pieces and the sense that we all knew that these might be his last looks.

And then, we're back at the Sussex cottage, planning the arrivals, renting the necessary places to stay, the food, the wine, etc. I manage to mask my intense depression by becoming the chauffeur. Everybody needed picking up at different times of the day and the night, some from Canada, some from the States, and some from France, so I am kept busy.

Everybody was having a great time, but there were two casualties.

Son Darcy, who was still not out of the addiction woods, was drinking himself into oblivion, and my dear sister, who had come directly from hospital, was in a state of utmost mental fragility. We feasted, cavorted on the beach, walked the Downs (a long line of gentle hills running along the south coast), and the four days flew by. Sadly, Eliza had to return to hospital in an ambulance and that weighed heavily on Jeremy. But otherwise, it meant a lot to him to connect to

Nicks children from left to right, Darcy, Carl, Stéphane and March with grandchildren

all the characters he'd heard so much about. As if that wasn't enough, I had had this brilliant idea: we would all leave Jeremy in peace and quiet for an Ashcroft/Hutchinson gathering in London. Which we did. It was another great reunion but all too much for my desperately depressed state of mind.

The next day I flew back to Canada. A few days later I landed in Salt Spring for a pre-rehearsal production meeting which convinced me, without a shadow of a doubt, that I wasn't equipped to do the show; full-blown depression, let's face it, is physically and mentally incapacitating. In the war, Churchill had to disappear for days to deal with his "Black Dogs"; it goes to show that no matter how intensely important a situation is, full-bore depression makes serious action and decision impossible. Leaving the show on the first day of rehearsal was the ultimate dereliction of duty, in my history of leaving shows. As always, "the show must go on," and the company valiantly took it on their shoulders without me.

Returning home to Enderby, defeated, I sat out most of that summer in that state. Would I ever do theatre again? Did I want to do theatre ever again? Chico made me go for walks. And there was one bright spot. I had this little sailing boat I'd bought years before when I went to Nanaimo to do a student production of Lysistrata. When I was still headed for Salt Spring, I'd thought, Why not bring it back to salt water? I really hadn't had much fun sailing the lakes up country. So, I'd hauled it down to Salt Spring—where I'd then got the crazy idea of the flotilla bringing the cast to shore as a prelude to The Chalk Circle. In in my "escape," I'd left the boat on its trailer in some parking lot.

I was too embarrassed and ashamed to go back to Salt Spring, but one of my occurring obsessive worries was what to do with the boat.

Summoning every ounce of courage, I phoned an old Caravan friend, Wendi, who lived on Salt Spring, to ask her if she could get the boat to some safe harbour. She brought a farmer friend of hers to give her a hand, whereupon he fell in love with The Queen Bee, for that was the name of the boat, and he was a beekeeper. He offered me a deal—in exchange for the boat, he would give me a free trip to Cuba with a group he was organizing to visit organic farms. What a deal! It was the first bright light on the horizon and turned out to be a joy and an inspiration.

As I write, Bernie Sanders is being attacked for praising the literacy program instigated by Fidel Castro. In Cuba, I experienced an amazing medical system, extraordinary schools, an organic farming system streaks ahead of North America, and a culture that celebrated its music, dance, and art. This wasn't an officially organized Soviet-style tour. We met many different kinds of people who could engage freely and speak their mind. Nobody we met was that enthusiastic about the party government, but they could all reflect on their history in a way which we in our free society don't.

The Cuban trip lifted my spirits and it felt like I was beginning to become a functional human being once more. Coming back from a walk across the Enderby Bridge that spans the Shuswap River, I'm looking at a somewhat dilapidated café perched on the river that has just been vacated. It has a beautiful balcony running all the way around it and a beautiful tower. And I have a flash: This is the Shuswap Swan Theatre. This could be articulated into a gorgeous festival theatre place. It's got parking. All those lovely balconies. I start to make enquiries because I think it might be affordable. Manic warning lights should be going off but, as always, the maniac remains oblivious!

And then Doug, my friend in Enderby, says, "Have you looked at the church next to my house?"

And I say, "No, but I'm not interested in the church."

And then the real estate agent, who helped me sell Tin Barn at the last minute, says, "Look. Ya gotta come and look at this building. This church."

"Oh, that church. The one Doug mentioned."

Off we go, and it blows my mind. Outside, it's a large nondescript nothing but you go in and the church proper is a wonderfully open, tall space—very adaptable from a theatrical point of view. It's got a great connection to audience and action and it's not super churchy. And it has library, rooms, offices, places for workshops and places for construction. It's got everything.

Ever since Peggy's death, I had had in mind the idea of an Ashcroft Company of Players, something my cousins and I had initially brainstormed. Now was the time, thought I. If there was a place that could accommodate all facets of a theatre operation, this was it. But Enderby alone couldn't support it—clearly it had to be a touring company. I had recently made friends with a producer/musician, John, who lived in Ashcroft BC and who was in the process of restoring the historic Ashcroft Opera House. If I was to secure the considerable finances—which would involve, at the least, putting my house and property up for collateral—I would need a sound business plan. In short, with the help of a couple of old friends, I developed a fully working plan. When the mind gathers wings in the bipolar state, the person suffering is completely unaware. Even though you'd think, from previous episodes, the sufferer would have learned their lesson. But all this visionary activity and super risky financial planning was launching me towards yet another manic episode. This time it was serious.

The sleepless nights began. I started losing track. I lost my dog. I lost a good guitar. I was beginning to hit walls. I lost my truck and spent nights looking for it, and when I did eventually find it, I blacked out on a busy highway and found myself careening and crunching down a steep embankment and onto some railroad tracks. A day or so later, meeting up with the agent who was coaxing me toward the sale, I persuaded him to take me to the local hospital for a check-up of my smashed-up back. I parlayed with the doctor in ER who said, "Wait a minute, let me just make a phone call." And it was clearly to my GP, who, alerted by the family, had been trying to persuade me to check into the psychiatric ward. I sensed that this was not going to lead to an assessment of my bruised back, and I was right. A burly RCMP collared me with the proverbial chokehold, dragged me through the ER staff, and told me to strip. Doing my best to maintain some semblance of dignity, I did so.

Presumably, because I can't remember anything afterwards, I was thumped with a sedative. I woke up in the Vernon Psychiatric Ward.

There is never much comfort in waking up in hospital—colourless walls, barely edible food—and when it's a psychiatric ward, the drugged patients wrapped in their own realities. But every cloud has a silvery lining, and for the first time, having gone through at least half a dozen psychiatrists, I was lucky enough to be seen by someone exceptional. She had fully researched my case history, she talked to Molly and March, and she had conversations with Jeremy. This had never been the usual approach. She immediately took me off the medications that I had been prescribed for the last twenty years and prescribed lithium, which I had always understood to be the go-to remedy for bipolar ever since I had read the seminal book on the condition, The Unquiet Mind. For some reason, no one had ever thought to try it out on me. But it worked, taking the edge off both ends of the spectrum, and has continued to do so.

During the time I was in the hospital, thanks to Molly, Chico had been recovered, and after a few weeks, Chico and I could resume life.

Nick and Jeremy walking the cliffs of Cuckmere

CHAPTER 26

Full Circle

B ut what was that life to be about? Lithium thus far had balanced my mind, but would it hold? My manic episodes had put paid to theatre ventures (the Hamlet in Montreal, the Chalk Circle in Salt Spring, and finally the pipedream of an Ashcroft Company). The terrors and errors of manic depression had taken its toll; I had lost the self confidence that had been the wellspring of creativity for most of my life. Then the horses—my rodeo with Fred Eaglesmith had fractured more than my T12 vertebra. It was wave upon wave of letting go. What could possibly fill the vacuum? I think Fate likes vacuums because it responded promptly. It being near the end of 2014, my father Jeremy's hundredth birthday loomed large, so off to England to meet the occasion.

Recently Jeremy had appeared on Desert Island Discs, a favorite BBC radio programme, where the host spins the invitees' favorite tunes, and chats, and it had begun a kind of late-in-life celebrity moment, where he was sought out for interviews and much attention. At the same time, he was writing a book *Jeremy Hutchinson's Case Histories* in partnership with Thomas Grant, a much younger Queens Counsel Barrister—an account of some of his most intriguing cases as a defence advocate. All this at the age of ninety-nine!

I had never encountered the delight and enthusiasm that Jeremy manifested in the preparations of his hundredth birthday party. His nephew, Jacob Rothschild (son of his sister Barbara), had offered to host the event at Spenser House, one of the grandest historical mansions in London. The guest list reflected all aspects of his life— family and friends and surviving colleagues— and there were many. On the actual day of his birthday, we were gathered at Lullington, Jeremy's beautiful cottage in Sussex, with Molly and March who had arrived for the birthday. In England when you turn one hundred, the Queen is supposed to send you a congratulatory card. We waited through a long breakfast to see if Her Majesty would remember and find the birthday boy's whereabouts . . . which she did, and Jeremy was thrilled. In many ways this was the height of irony as traditionally the Hutchinsons are republicans. Our ancestor John Hutchinson, Member of Parliament for Nottingham, sat on the jury that tried Charles I and executed him after the civil war, and when the monarchy was eventually restored, John was incarcerated in seriously

Jeremy receiving a card from the Queen for his 100th Bithday

bleak conditions until his death. Many other Hutchinsons fled the country to America and the West Indies.

For the next three years Jeremy filled my life. The hundred-year celebrations and the publishing of his book were the high points before the gradual deterioration of his faculties, bringing tougher moments, but often tinged with humour. His mind would hang in till the end. One such memorable moment, occurred when his doctor was trying to persuade him to take some medications, getting him seriously riled. As she beat a hasty retreat towards the front door, Jeremy in full voice cried, "I don't want antibiotics. I want a pill to let me slip away!"

The time had come for carers—fortunately, fantastic carers who could relate to Jeremy, his humour and zest for life, even as it was disappearing. We were settled now in Lullington, as beautiful a spot as you could wish for, nestled into the Downs and looking down a river valley, the Cuckmere, that led to the sea. It was on the cliffs overlooking the Cuckmere River running into the sea that Jeremy had proposed to Peggy in 1940, and after the war they had considered buying one of the three coastguard cottages that perched precariously on the edge of the crumbly chalk cliffs. In the end they decided it was too risky, but nonetheless the spot had always been a precious and favorite target of walks, swims, and rock skimming.

As one by one his faculties faded, his heart continued to beat metronomically, and we remembered that many years before he'd had a pacemaker inserted. Of course, reminded of that, he wanted it switched off. I hunted down the doc who had put it in and despite all the pressure we could bring, he refused—said we were the first to request such a procedure and though it would take but a few minutes on a computer, he could not risk the consequences (as in familial disputes etc.). So the battle with life that would not let go continued, much to my father's irritation.

Eventually Jeremy won and died, as we all hope to do, in his bed in the wee hours of the morning—the dog watch.

Near Lullington in the dim and distant past lived members of the Bloomsburys. Central to this extraordinary group of writers, artists, and thinkers were the two sisters—Virginia Woolf and Vanessa Bell— who lived there with their husbands. My grandparents Jack and Mary were close friends. A half-hour walk from Lullington was a small flint-stone church in the village of Berwick, that had been frescoed by Vanessa and her roommate Duncan Grant. It was there that we held Jeremy's funeral. We did our best to make a cheerful event, climaxing in all of us full-throatedly singing what had become Jeremy's favorite song, "Que sera sera," with a last verse he had demanded I write:

"Then I got older, a hundred and two, I asked my son what the hell do I do? Do I go on and on and on? He said "It's up to you! . . . Que sera sera" . . .

As night fell, our family and some close friends went to Cuckmere, bringing with us Jeremy's ashes. We made paper boats— some hastily made by kids, some perfectly folded and sea ready, by March and Molly—then we filled them with the ashes. Some of us held kerosene torches on long sticks to light their way. We launched them in the river, where they bobbed about until they found the current and finally sailed out to sea, disappearing into the waves and darkness.

So ends my return to my roots. Some English friends asked if I would stay. And though in many ways it had been fulfilling to be in England for more than a brief holiday, in the final analysis, the underlying reasons I'd left in the first place, still held. The fundamental class structure was still there. And just as when I was a boy, being the son of Dame Peggy Ashcroft and Lord Jeremy Hutchinson was inescapable. No! Back to the life I had built in the wilds of Canada, however higgledy-piggledy.

One thing I hadn't paid much attention to during the roller-coaster of looking after a dying dad, was that my mind had remained steady throughout. Glory be to lithium! If lithium works for you (for some it just doesn't) it can truly be a miracle: the mind maintains equilibrium and there are no palpable side effects. Of course, there are moments when I miss the shimmering clarity and inspiration of the manic seesaw but the Black Dogs of Depression are never fun and never worth it.

As for theatre, today. It needs to re-find the magic of the mask and the dramatic power of disguise, as it struggles for survival in the face of entertainment that isolates its audience, streaming its dramas and social media into individual lonely living rooms. Perhaps when Climate Armageddon comes, and screens and internets go down, we shall see the rebirth of the most fulfilling form of social connection—theatre!

And maybe, just maybe, the power of working horses could be re-discovered, just as it was by the caravan theatres of yesteryear, pulling their loads from field to field and road to road.

One day when the oil barrels have all dripped dry
And the nights are seen to grow colder
They'll beg for your strength, your gentle power,
Your noble grace and your bearing
And you'll strain once again to the sound of the gulls
In the wake of the deep plow shearing

Jethro Tull "Heavy Horses"

From the day I sat atop Mr. Bishop's plow horse at the age of three, to the many times I helped a newborn foal to find its mother's teat, to my buddy Snake falling dead at my feet, horses have left me with more memories and food for thought than I can count.